LIVING
WITH
WINE

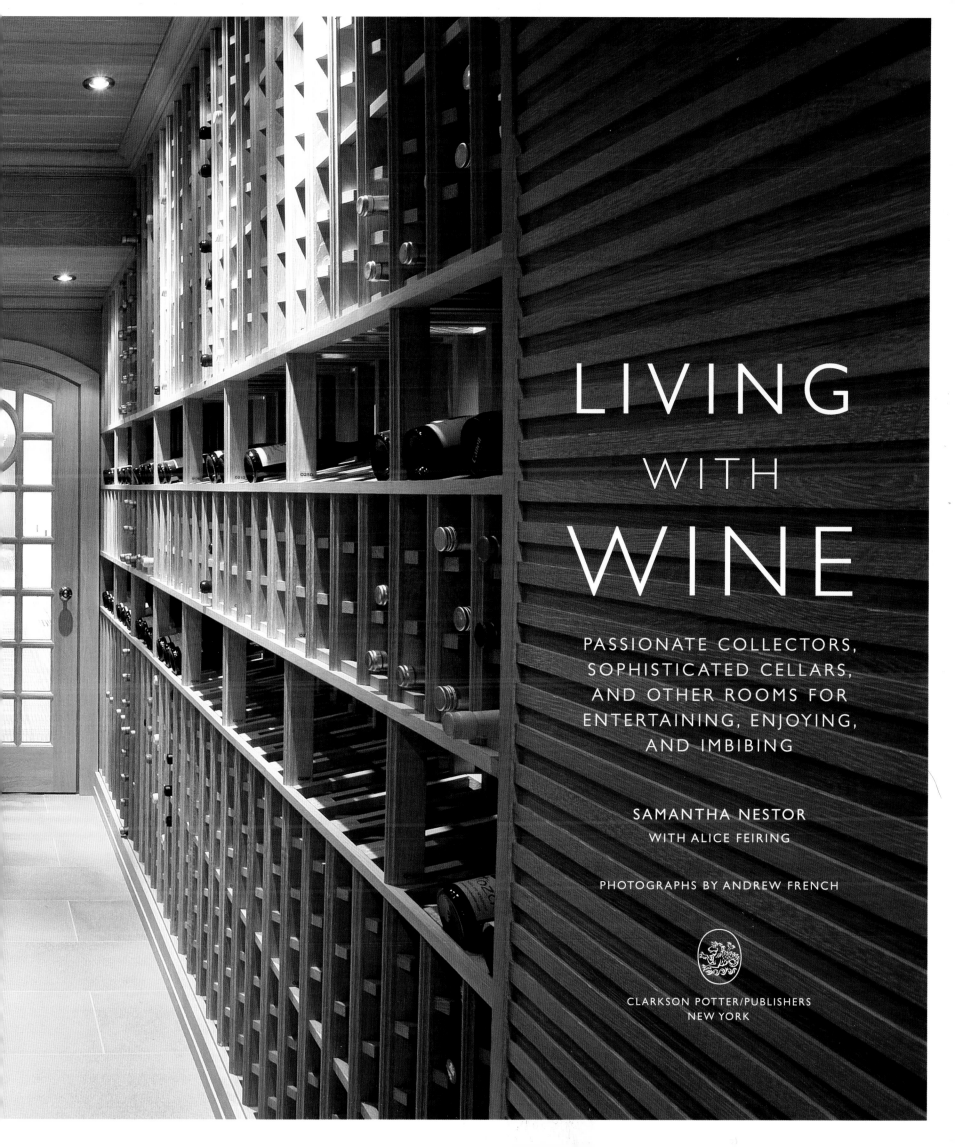

LIVING
WITH
WINE

PASSIONATE COLLECTORS,
SOPHISTICATED CELLARS,
AND OTHER ROOMS FOR
ENTERTAINING, ENJOYING,
AND IMBIBING

SAMANTHA NESTOR

WITH ALICE FEIRING

PHOTOGRAPHS BY ANDREW FRENCH

CLARKSON POTTER/PUBLISHERS
NEW YORK

Published in the United States by CLARKSON POTTER/PUBLISHERS, an imprint of the CROWN PUBLISHING GROUP,
a division of RANDOM HOUSE, INC., New York.
www.crownpublishing.com
www.clarksonpotter.com

CLARKSON POTTER is a trademark and POTTER with colophon is a registered trademark of Random House, Inc.

DESIGN BY JENNIFER K. BEAL DAVIS

PHOTOGRAPHS BY ANDREW FRENCH, EXCEPT ON PAGE 113 (ABOVE RIGHT) BY FRANCIS C. GRAY III; PAGE 179 AND 180 (ABOVE LEFT)
BY ANDY KATZ PHOTOGRAPHY; PAGES 166 (ABOVE RIGHT) AND 198–203 BY BEN BENOIT. POSTPRODUCTION BY DUN DIGITAL.

Library of Congress Cataloging-in-Publication Data
Nestor, Samantha.
Living with wine / Samantha Nestor.
  p.   cm.
1. Wine cellars.   I. Title.
TP548.5.A6N47   2009
641.2'2—dc22   2008051522

978-0-307-40789-4

Printed in China

10 9 8 7

First Edition

FOR FAY

CONTENTS

INTRODUCTION

IT HAS BEEN SAID "Where there is no wine there is no love."*

Today, America's love of wine has spurred a collecting and entertaining phenomenon. As more people join the wine-collecting family, their desire to make wine part of their lives has facilitated the creation of magnificent spaces. No longer are wine cellars the little dungeons that a staff member visited to select a bottle to bring to the guests upstairs. Now the wine cellar is part of an entertaining matrix that marries luxurious design aesthetics and ingenious storage solutions. The results are so inviting that they encourage their owners (and guests) to spend meaningful time there. This new addition to the cultured home has become the place to entertain and imbibe, and it often commands surprisingly large amounts of real estate.

When I first started developing *Living with Wine*, I found collectors most intriguing because the majority of the objects they amass will (eventually) be consumed. I learned that these passionate individuals loved to share the story of how they discovered "the" bottle. Or perhaps they would choose to chat about a journey they had taken to acquire a certain wine before they uncorked it so we could enjoy it together. And then they would tell me about the cellars. Thus began an ebb and flow, a coming and going of bottles; the stories of sharing, of entertaining, and of building the space that housed prized possessions. Cellars were once little more than passive "caves" or holes in the ground and now, thanks to creative interior designers, architects, and builders, the cellar has become a new area for opulence and revelry. Of course, cellars must function with proper temperature and humidity control, but now the spaces are lovely to look at and reveal their owners' personalities and their designers' ingenuity.

*EURIPIDES, circa B.C. 480–406.

Americans love their wine. According to the Wine Institute, over the past ten years, wine consumption in the United States has gone from 510 million gallons in 1997 to 745 million gallons in 2007. That's a lot of juice! Wine collecting isn't merely relegated to a boys' club of businessmen or wealthy heirs. The group featured within this book is diverse: It includes women and men, people with backgrounds in environmental activism, fashion, finance, restaurant development, law, film production, and television. What all of these individuals have in common is that they have turned their collecting passion into a haven in their homes. The wine cellar is a place where they escape and entertain, tell stories, and share their wine.

Living with Wine showcases thirty extraordinary wine cellars and collections and shows all facets of the wine cellar, the tasting room, and the storage areas, including different solutions for generous and limited square footage. It includes cellars from large estates to urban apartments, from the small state of Rhode Island to the great wine-producing state of California. The book is divided into five parts: the Entertaining Pair's Lair, the Gentleman's Haven, the Sybarite's Sanctuary, the Modernist Refuge, and Urban Retreats and Inspiring Spaces, which displays three fine commercial spaces that have influenced residential cellar design. Some individuals profiled here are just beginning their wine journey, that enviable first blush of wine collecting; others have been amassing their cellars for decades.

Cellars are indeed emerging from the basement and being designed strategically into or around the central entertaining spaces of the home. Many of these cellars were created to blend seamlessly with the rest of the home. The owners and designers collaborated closely to ensure the cellars would

address the desire of owners such as television and radio personality Ryan Seacrest, who said, "I wanted the wine-cellar design to be on par with the rest of my home. I wanted it functional, to the point, yet personal and meaningful."

Some of the cellars included contain green solutions, and one opitimizes a commitment to green design.

Even though I currently reside in Connecticut, my fifteen years as a New Yorker make me think like an urban dweller. Some of the most passionate collectors I know are New Yorkers, and wine storage is as important to them as it is to those on Napa estates. So I set out to find some smart designs for petite spaces. The result is savvy solutions that are also ideal for starter collections where the goal is to make the most of the space available in order to artfully display and organize a budding collection. Clever design solutions are not limited to residential projects. Also included are award-winning commercial wine cellars that offer the homeowner a different form of inspiration from restaurants, hotels, and private clubs.

Living with Wine allows readers to join the wine-collecting family and reflects America's passion for wine. I invite you to join me and wine writer Alice Feiring as we traverse the country exploring thirty jaw-dropping wine cellars. Come with us as we visit these wonderful spaces, view enticing collections, and meet inspiring oenophiles. Whether you are building a cellar or just want to imagine one, sit down with *Living with Wine*, uncork a favorite bottle, relax, and enjoy the stories. *Living with Wine* is about loving life.

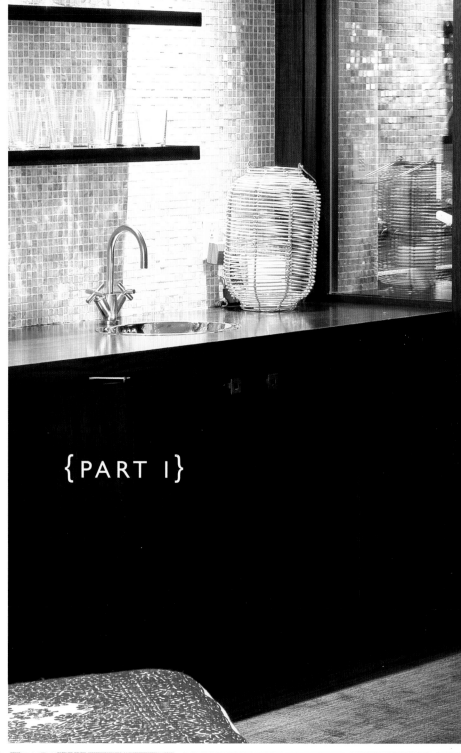

{PART 1}

THE ENTERTAINING PAIR'S LAIR

The owners of these cellars could never be satisfied with musty rooms tucked away or inaccessible subterranean dens. Their wine-storage solutions are strategically knit into or spun around the central entertaining spaces of the home. And in some cases, they *are* the stand-alone, primary entertaining space. Similar to the kitchen, a room once shuttered behind swinging doors, the wine cellar is taking a place of prominence. These "cellars" are functional, accessible, and social, broadening the wine experience into a welcoming one for guests as well as the owner. Practically speaking, these collectors—for whom drinking wine is an everyday affair and a way of life—see their "cellars" as their favorite spot to decompress.

Such spaces are ideal for families and singles alike. Some cellars have reinterpreted the living room, others have become part of a groovy entertainment complex or a sophisticated tasting library. What used to be standardized is now marvelously varied, from racking styles to interior design and the accessories within. The owners of these wonderful retreats are bound together by their desire to share their passion.

VIEW TO A VINEYARD

NEW CANAAN, CONNECTICUT

THE KENDS' NEO-GEORGIAN PALLADIAN HILLTOP HOUSE needed plenty of work before the couple could claim it as their own. At purchase the interiors were too ornate to meld with their more urban aesthetic. The columns on the front of the house had to be removed, as did the embellishments on the twelve fireplaces.

In order to achieve the sublime transformation they hired Diamond Baratta, the firm known for executing the design of Meryl Streep's character's apartment in the film *The Devil Wears Prada*. The Kends now feel at home. Their living quarters is just what they had envisioned: an environment influenced by the mid-century Italian modernist Gio Ponti. Husband Peter Kend jokes, "It's like a Martian spaceship!" The downstairs, dominated by the winding and twisting wine cellar designed by David Spon, also reflects this same whimsical aesthetic. However, this is no spaceship—unless the Martian has a penchant for Trocken Beren Auslese and all things Riesling. "I'll come out of the closet," Peter Kend admits. "I love white wines."

Kend was an eight-year-old when his wine curiosity was piqued. The year was 1972, and the scene was the *SS France*, upon which his family was making the move to England. "My father knew nothing about wine. In fact, he didn't even drink. I remember he asked the traditional sommelier—complete with a *tastevin* hanging about his neck—to hook him up with something great. My father let me sample. From then on, wine was always around the table. My dad segued from one whisky sour a year to one glass of wine a week."

As a teenager, Kend began to train as a chef, which led him deeper into the well of wine's mysteries. Thanks to his father's friends with extensive cellars, he cut his teeth on the famed 1961 Bordeaux vintage. "It's one of the vintages I can taste blind." But, please, he insists, don't confuse him with a Bordeaux lover. "I find them a little monochromatic. I still don't understand Petrus."

Now, in his mid-forties, Kend—who has bounced between derivatives trading and being a restaurateur—believes strongly in the wine and food connection. "It's all about that synergy," he says. "They need to be supporting characters for each other, and the reason for my white-wine love is that I find it, and especially a Riesling, does this best." At this point he has seven thousand bottles of those beloved whites as well as

significant red holdings. A tenth of the collection is in magnums.

Having already created one cellar in the past with David Spon, Kend called him in on this project as well. This time around, with the benefit of experience, the homeowner was prepared with a list of new needs. "For that first cellar I hadn't as yet discovered my love of large-format bottles. I didn't have enough crate storage. I wanted several rooms to help create more efficient organization. And I wanted top-of-the-line computer technology so I could easily track the movement of bottles," Kend adds.

A third of the basement—1,200 feet—was co-opted and transformed into a complex jumble of curves, angles, and bins, but the overall effect remains straightforward. The logic is achieved by Spon's design and Kend's personal organizational skills. The cellar door opens onto a long hallway. On one side is floor-to-ceiling racking. On the other are windows that look out onto the tasting room, and beyond that, huge photographs of vineyards that are so lifelike they provoke a double take. Off the hallway are the twisty and curvy rooms for storage: one for crates, one for magnums, a fanciful U-shaped room for red and white Burgundies, a room full of diamond bins, and some rooms that fit up to five hundred bottles. To avoid courting the disaster that could easily happen with bins—bottle breakage—Spon incorporated a slight upward tilt that keeps the bottles in place.

OVERLEAF: Solid white cerused oak with well-defined grain abounds throughout the cellar.

ABOVE: Kend says, "I don't drink California too often, but if there's one thing that Napa Cabernet is good for, it's grilled meat."

ABOVE RIGHT: The downstairs, dominated by the winding wine cellar, echoes the whimsical aesthetic of the rest of the house.

Solid white oak abounds throughout the cellar, in the sturdy bins as well as in the curved slatted ceiling. The grain is well defined; in fact, it pops out. Kend requested this particular look. To achieve it, a process called "ceruse" was employed, a pickling that defines the white in the grain. The process requires a series of seven painstaking steps. "We have cerused oak upstairs in the house and I asked David to use it for the racking, so we kept the continuity. If David knew what he was going to be in for, he'd never have said yes. In fact, he never stops reminding me what torture that process was for him," Kend says.

While the cellar is definitely Kend's domain, his wife had an active hand in stocking it. "At the beginning of our marriage—nineteen years now—she didn't really get the wine thing, until she read Kermit Lynch's seminal book, *Adventures on the Wine Route*. She fell in love with the section on the northern Rhône producer Chave. She offered, 'I'll make a deal. You just buy what you want every year and I'll buy one case of Chave red and one of white.' Now Chave's Hermitage is probably my single largest red-wine holding and, by the way, that Chave Blanc has got to be one of the best whites on the planet."

While Kend also has some California wines stocked, he makes no secret about being an Old World drinker. "I'm pretty sure all people who get serious about wine end up preferring them. Like, at the beginning, when I drank California Pinot, it was Williams Selyem; now it's Burgundy and Ponsot. It also doesn't get better than Lebanon's

ABOVE: Off the hallway are curvy rooms for storage: one for crates; one for magnums; a fanciful U-shape for red and white Burgundies; and a room full of diamond bins, some that fit up to five hundred bottles.

ABOVE RIGHT: Spon incorporated a slight upward tilt to keep the bottles in place in their diamond bins.

ABOVE: Kend believes strongly in the wine and food connection. "It's all about that synergy," he says. "They need to be supporting characters for each other."

OPPOSITE: Kend frequents the 30-inch Apple screen at the end of the long corridor, where his new toy, the software program Cellar Advisor, makes his wine-tracking easy.

Château Musar," he says, referring to the iconic, rich, and sunny Lebanese wine. "And I have them all in big bottles," he says with a good deal of excitement.

Kend says it seems as if he buys wine every day and as a result he spends a lot of time in his cellar, physically maintaining the collection and cataloguing new acquisitions. He makes frequent use of the 30-inch Apple screen at the end of the long corridor because the computer is loaded up with one of Kend's new toys, Cellar Advisor, a software program that makes his wine tracking extremely easy.

"The minute I buy wine, I enter the bottles into the program. There are three bar-code readers in the cellar as well. Tracking the ins and outs couldn't be easier."

Also putting a smile on this trained chef's face is the dining area just outside the cellar. "I never understood having a dining area/tasting area inside the cellar, because it's so cold!" But Kend desired the ability to dine close to bottle access, so right outside the temperature-controlled door is a cook-worthy fireplace. Because it is a basement,

after all, he was trying to figure out how to cozy up the environment to make the area a place one would want to dine in. Then a big idea struck him. He bought some of photographer Sarah Matthews's vineyard shots, blew them up to life-size, and now when he's grilling steaks, his guests sit at the table looking over those trompe l'oeil vineyards. And would he be serving Riesling with those steaks?

"Not really," he says. "I'd bring out a highly respected Ann Colgin Cabernet. I don't drink California too often, but if there's one thing that Napa Cabernet is good with, it's grilled meat."

OPPOSITE: A "wall of wine," created by Jean Shin, signals the entrance to the cellar from the main living quarters. Shin assembled the installation onsite.

ABOVE: On one side is floor-to-ceiling racking. On the other are windows that look out to the tasting room where huge photographs of vineyards are so lifelike, they provoke a double-take. • Kend enjoys throwing dinner parties close to bottle access. Guests dine in the adjacent tasting room overlooking Sarah Matthews's monumental photographs of vineyards.

CELLAR SNAPSHOT

CAPACITY: 7,000 BOTTLES

DUJAC CLOS DE LA ROCHE

TRIMBACH CLOS ST. HUNE

JEAN-LOUIS CHAVE HERMITAGE

RIDGE MONTE BELLO

DOMAINE WEINBACH PINOT GRIS ALTENBOURG CUVEE LAURENCE

DOMAINE DES BAUMARD QUARTS DE CHAUME

OBJECTS OF DESIRE:
ARTWORK AND COLLECTIBLES IN THE WINE CELLAR

The wine-mad tend to want to decorate their space not only with bottles but also with other wine accoutrements. From labels with infinitely varied illustrations to funnels, bottle stoppers, and other functional objects that become design objects of desire, the trappings often show up in wine cellars as another kind of collection.

Many collectors save used corks for their sentimental value. The catalyst could be the desire to preserve something from a memorable event or important date or the desire to create a sort of three-dimensional catalog of favorite wines. Whether given pride of place in a magnificent wine cellar or perched in a glass bowl on a nightstand, corks are small and easy to save. For those who are lucky enough to have cellars, a cork collection can be turned into a work of art, as in the Weston, Connecticut, cellar designed by Celerie Kemble, where a large glass amphora holds the past year's indulgences. In Susie Turner's Narragansett beauty, the entire cellar's focal point is a table with cork details showcased beneath glass.

Wine bottles may be an obvious way to decorate a cellar, but wine sophisticates have also found interesting ways to draw attention to them. Ken Ziffren's living-room wine cellar uses empty bottles of sentimental value to dot the windowsills as decoration. For his entry, Peter Kend commissioned artist Jean Shin to build a wine wall out of recycled wine bottles. The effect is dazzling, and the refracted light guides the visitor to the wine cellar. One oenophile took bottle display to a new level—having the company Studium create a monumental bottle mosaic of assorted marble, limestone, and onyx at the entrance to the cellar. Says Studium's president, David Meitus, "We developed the design based on the bottle itself, taking great care to capture every detail of the label, the bottle contour even as we adjusted the scale. The original mosaic is created entirely by hand."

Most wine cellars don't have windows because of possible damage to the wine. Many owners get creative trying to find substitutes for the light, color, and visual variety that views provide. Peter Kend purchased vineyard photographs by Sarah Matthews, blew them up life-size, and hung them to surround the tasting/dining area adjacent to the storage space. The effect is like being swept away to Napa.

The chosen artwork can also be more sentimental than decorative, as in Lou Kapcsándy's cellar, which is punctuated by his sister's decorative paintings of the family coat of arms, arbors, and grapevines. Rick Ryan purchased art from local talents and festivals for his Weston, Massachusetts, cellar.

Not to be limited to the physical bottle, some collectors also hoard and display the ritualistic tools of wine tasting and drinking. For example, Tom Strauss has adorned his tasting room with a variety of wine paraphernalia. His sideboards are filled with antique decanters, elegant English funnels, corkscrews, and one-of-a-kind teardrop stemware. The finishing touch is a thousand-liter barrel from France, its head embedded in the stone wall.

The options for art in a wine cellar are as diverse as the group of oenophiles themselves.

MOROCCAN MOODS

THE YEAR WAS 1990. THE PLACE WAS NAPA. The purpose was a Goldman Sachs team-building retreat. And one of the results was a wine-obsessed couple. "When we were confronted with our first Opus and Caymus, we couldn't resist," Lisa says.

From then on, collecting and drinking wine was one of Lisa and Jeff's chief obsessions. When they moved from the illustrious Dakota apartment building on New York's Upper West Side to their present abode in northwestern Connecticut, they knew it was time to get serious and give the wines a proper place to shine. Their modest collection had grown from a few easy-to-deal-with cases into a serious storage issue.

But before they could address their wine needs, they had to install their formal furnishings into the antique house, a low-ceilinged, wooden-beamed affair that looked part pre-Revolutionary, part 1800s pub. Interior designer Celerie Kemble of New York and Palm Beach–based Kemble Interiors played with color to fit the couple's formal French furniture into the New England framework. The couple was happy with the results but everyone involved in the project, from the family to Kemble to architect Peter Cadoux, agrees that the fun

really started when they had to turn the basement into a wine-friendly entertainment complex.

Cadoux reports that the space—which was to hold a collection of rooms that would also include a theater—was a drywall dig-out. At one-half the footprint of the house, it wasn't very large. There was an entry from both the garage and the main house above. "Having it on the same level as the garage was going to make it perfectly easy for loading crates of wine into the cellar," he says.

Even more important than the ease of having the garage at hand is the convenience of having their prized collection of wine close by. Kemble says, "Having that collection of wine there was perfect. A presentation of wine changes the mood of a space and becomes its heart. If it weren't for the focal point of the wine, the other rooms would seem like a collection of disconnected rooms. The wine coalesces everything."

As for finding the design theme, Kemble claims it was a cinch. "Before the couple segued into parenthood they were travel-hungry peripatetics," she says. Two of Lisa and Jeff's favorite destinations had been Spain and Morocco. Moroccan wine didn't exactly hit a home run

with them, but the Moroccan aesthetic did, and they wanted their fantasy cellar to bring them back there. They found a design book, *Houses & Palaces of Andalusia* by Patricia Espinosa de los Monteros and Francesco Venturi, and placed it in Kemble's hands, indicating, "This please!"

Something a bit mysterious and awash in rich jewel tones was called for. To begin with, the existing rickety staircase needed to be demolished and was replaced with the ebony scissor stairs, which now zigzag down to an altered reality. Saturated burgundy wallpaper in a trellis-like print—almost bordello-like—lines the walls and, down below, the North

African influences emerge with the arched doorways, heavy, carved-wooden doors, Moorish chairs, wrought iron, and high-polish ebony, walnut, and copper accents.

Lisa says she loves that first glimpse of wines through the frame of glass set into the wall. The window sits above two adorable vintage chairs the couple found at a local antiques store. The chairs, though American, have that North African appeal and lend the space a hint of Moroccan flair. With the warm lighting, it almost seems like the beach in the late afternoon. Architect Cadoux remarked that lighting was a priority. "You've got to get lighting essentials absolutely right

OVERLEAF: A new ebony scissor stairs was installed that zigzags down from the living quarters into a wine-friendly entertainment complex in the cellar.

ABOVE, LEFT TO RIGHT: Mosaic tile was set on its reverse side to give a rough-and-tumble look. A local artisan did tactile encaustic work on the walls. • Marking the transition from the bar to

the wine's safe room is a found object, a Mexican reproduction of a Spanish wrought-iron door, which, architect Cadoux said, took a bit of maneuvering and some shaving to fit.

OPPOSITE: The space is punctuated by saturated burgundy wallpaper in a trellislike print and with North African accents such as arched doorways; heavy, carved wooden doors; and Moorish chairs.

The entrance to the compact wine cellar is a jewel box of a wet bar with a copper farmhouse sink.

in a subterranean space. You can never think, *Get me out of here into better light!*"

Kemble agreed with that perspective. Her effort was geared toward transforming the cellar into a place that felt well inhabited. "I went to lengths to avoid that just-moved-in feel." She said that too much repetition of materials, such as too much of one kind of wood, reads as "new." To avoid that pitfall she employed a wide array of textures and rich materials—like the wallpaper, the rugs, the limestone, and the copper—and layered them in for some serious coziness.

The entrance to the rectangular, compact wine cellar is a stunning jewel box of a wet bar, so spectacular it shares billing with the cellar. Like an irresistible magnet for the eye, the copper farmhouse sink shimmers. Its bright liveliness contrasts with the darkly polished wood. Marking the transition from the bar to the wine's safe room is a found object, a Mexican reproduction of a Spanish wrought-iron door, which, Cadoux said, took a bit of maneuvering and some shaving to fit into a seal. Inside the room the bottles are laid out in a straightforward and functional way, but

ABOVE, LEFT TO RIGHT: The space is a collection of rooms that also includes a home theater adjacent to the cellar • Further warming the room are mirrors, lighting from the wrought-iron fixtures, and a piano. • Kemble layered the space and created intimacy with a wide array of textures and rich materials such as the wallpaper, the rugs, the limestone, and the copper.

extraordinary detail brings them to life. Pinkish gold Jerusalem stone flooring brings the Mediterranean feeling home. Further warming the room are mirrors and wrought-iron lighting fixtures. The architect used tile creatively, too. For example, mosaic tile was set on its reverse side to give a rough-and-tumble look. A local artisan did truly tactile encaustic work on the walls. It begs to be touched, as do the bottles.

Lisa and Jeff welcome their friends with Opus One and Caymus from their first buying sprees. Today, they are crazy about the wines of Spain. Their philosophy is: Drink today, because no one knows what will happen tomorrow; thus, they're not scouting wines for investment. That means they're comfortable shopping both at high-end wine stores and at the local Stew Leonard's, where a favorite salesperson might give them a call to say, "You know that Alion you like so much? Well then, you must taste some of the new wines from Monsant. We just got them in." Right now, they're thinking they should slow down on the buying; the amount of wine they have seems staggering to them. But Lisa says, "I remember thinking, *seven hundred bottles? Never!* And look what happened!"

CELLAR SNAPSHOT

CAPACITY: 1,000 BOTTLES
OPUS ONE
CAYMUS
ALION
VEGA SICILIA

LEFT: The window sits above two adorable vintage chairs the couple found at a local antiques store. The chairs, though American, have a North African appeal and a Moroccan flair.

A MAP OF ITALY

NORTH CALDWELL, NEW JERSEY

CAROL AND MARK SCUDIERY TAKE THE
ITALIAN STYLE OF LIVING SERIOUSLY. They
reside in their new home, built to invoke the feeling of
an Italian villa, in New Jersey, about forty minutes from
Manhattan. Both husband and wife are fantastic cooks
and fanatics about wining and dining. Their enormous
kitchen has marble countertops that seem to stretch into
the horizon. Punctuating various surfaces are photographs depicting friends eating and drinking in the
couple's home and in Italy, where the Scudierys
frequently vacation.

While other people place the wine cellar in a luxurious trio with the gym and media room, here at the
Scudiery residence the cellar helps complete a different
kind of entertaining complex—the kitchen and dining
room. Placing the cellar within easy reach of these two
rooms was essential for Scudiery because, as he says, "I
can go into the wine cellar six times during a dinner to
choose different wines. It really needs to be accessible.
The fact that the cellar isn't in fact *in* the cellar was one
of my needs."

To get to the cellar, one passes through the stunning
tasting room, with its classically inspired hand-painted
murals and ceilings, and careful plasterwork. Full
windows offer gorgeous views of the garden, conducive
to setting the mood for sampling from Scudiery's
extensive assortment of artisanal grappas after dinner,
or a sparkler before. A small hallway, flanked by glassware and grappa bottles, leads into the sacred room
where he houses his wines.

In the '70s, Scudiery, a man who has been described
as having a certain Al Pacino quality about him, was
starting out in pharmaceuticals. In those days he had
nothing against popping open the Lancers and Mateus
for his daily tipples. Horrified, his Italian barbers took
matters in hand and invited him to lunch at a New York
City Italian restaurant, Parioli Romanissimo. "They told
me we were going to drink a 1955 Biondi-Santi," he
reminisces, referring to the iconic Brunello di
Montalcino.

The taste of that wine changed his vinous future. No
more fizzy, commercial wines for him. "From then on,"
he says, "when I did buy wine, it was better quality!"

His collecting spark ignited years later when, in
1996, he started his own business and had the financial
means to buy without having to bother looking at price

tags. In retrospect, there was one problem—he looked at points. "I followed [Robert] Parker," he offers, as an explanation as to why he still has some bottles of high-octane Australian, Californian, and Bordeaux wines on his Cellar Tracker spreadsheet. But more and more he found that that style of wine did not suit him. He wondered if something was the matter with his palate. "You know," he says, "at one point I thought that all of those big, fruit-forward wines tasted generic."

After reading *The Accidental Connoisseur,* a book by Lawrence Osborne that addressed what made one wine differ from another, he had a second wine epiphany. "Up until that point I hadn't even heard the word *'terroir',*" Scudiery says. He's mostly an Old World kind of guy with the lion's share of his wine collection in traditionally made Italians, but he has expanded his repertoire to include some French wines, such as southern Rhônes and Burgundies. "When I compared Pinot Noir from California to French Burgundies I was astounded. That's when it came together for me. Burgundies had a clarity and purity. There's nothing the matter with domestic Pinot," he continues. "I just don't find them interesting. At this point, I've sold most of them off. Those that remain go to my children, who are quite happy to drink them up."

OVERLEAF: "The fact that the cellar isn't in fact *in* the cellar was one of my needs," says Scudiery.

ABOVE: Scudiery admits that what he likes best about his cellar are the wines. • Scudiery's home was built to evoke an Italian villa.

OPPOSITE: "Mark's cellar is like a map of Italy," said Zinser. "His cellar is organized into regions." • A pair of frosted-over windows flank the room. • Once in the stem of the cellar, the literary atmosphere is enforced with the sumptuous, warm African mahogany, matched to the windows and doors used elsewhere in the house.

The L-shaped cellar, with its tumbled marble floors, suggests the intimacy of a rare-book room, but with bottles instead of volumes. The bottom of the "L" boasts substantial space for bulk wine storage. Once in the "stem" of the cellar, the literary atmosphere is enforced with sumptuous, warm African mahogany, matched to that used for the windows and doors elsewhere in the house. The objective for the designer, Lee Zinser, is always to tie the other elements from the house into the cellar so there is flow. "We want people to move from one space to the other without feeling any disparity," he says.

Unless lighting functions as art, Zinser prefers hiding fixtures in furniture and using natural light when possible. Here, flanking the room, two frosted-over windows add to the intimate warmth. Marking each section are selected bottles standing up like sentries. These serve as a visual catalogue. "Mark's cellar is like a map of Italy," says Zinser. "It's organized into regions, so a bottle of Barolo stands up to announce that this section is Piedmont. A bottle of Abruzzo stands up over there to say, "Here are the Montepulcianos."

"There are so many aspects of this cellar that I love. One is the access from the kitchen; [another] is the seamless dovetailing to the rest of the house," Scudiery says, taking a moment to pull out some of his favorite wines, such as Quintarelli Amarone, or eccentric beauties made in amphorae, like Radikon and Gravner. For a moment he gets distracted. "And I just love old-fashioned classics, such as Emidio Pepe from Montepulciano d'Abruzzo." Then he muses, "You know, at the end of the day, what I like most are the wines."

OPPOSITE: The bottom of the "L" boasts substantial space for bulk wine storage. Marking each section are selected bottles standing up like sentries. These serve as a visual catalogue.

CELLAR SNAPSHOT

CAPACITY: 3,500
QUINTARELLI AMARONE
RADIKON
GRAVNER
EMIDIO PEPE
MONTEPULCIANO D'ABRUZZO

THE FIRST FLUSH

WATERMILL, NEW YORK

"I'M A COMPLETE WINE NOVICE," PATRICK MCMAHON HAS NO TROUBLE CONFESSING. That certainly was not an obstacle once he decided that his new home would have a wine cellar. His business partner, a wine fanatic, had taken him under his wing, and obviously he is off to a terrific start. "If I had to say what my special bottle was, it would have to be Château Haut-Brion," McMahon says.

Without a doubt, there are more special bottles for him to discover down the line. McMahon, a principal at a leading investment management firm, is at an enviable stage for a collector—the beginning, when the experience is so similar to falling in love for the first time; the world is open and the first flush of excitement is hard to beat. But McMahon is taking his wine-shopping sprees in stride. As he heads up a hedge fund, he's used to taking risks, but when it comes to buying his wines, he keeps his feet on the ground. "I'm not about being a collector," he says. "It's all about people for me—who makes the wine and who I'm sharing it with."

McMahon is an avid entertainer. Friends fill his new Watermill, Long Island, home every weekend. They make lavish use of his subterranean playground, which includes one of the highest-end home theaters in the country (complete with D-Box seating and massagers), a billiards table, a wine-tasting lounge area delightfully warmed by a fireplace, and the wine cave that is now stocked with two thousand bottles.

Like his attraction to Haut-Brion, McMahon has an intuitive connection to great design. "I don't have the vocabulary to articulate exactly why I do or don't like a wine, or to say why I do or do not resonate with design. But I do know what I like," McMahon asserts. "Interior design can provoke strong feelings. Some places are inviting and some are not. My living space and the cellar had to be inviting."

He also wanted to distill his vision of the Hamptons into his home. "Many homes in this area are built to Hamptons expectations, and I wanted something that respected the traditional nature of the area with a more modern flair and edge." Seeking that special point of view in his 6,400-square-foot home, he hired Marie Aiello Design Studio to bring form to his aspirations. The vision for the wine cellar was to make it part of the milieu of the entire house, that movement between one space and another should be seamless. She and builder

The entrance to McMahon's
Hamptons estate is punctuated
by a custom gate designed by
Aiello

The bar area is washed with a glittering mosaic of tile called Honey Onyx Mosaic. The effect continues into the wine cellar, appearing on the interior wall and around a column.

Lee Zinser shared some similar priorities. "I loved working with Lee Zinser. His ability to understand and embrace the tone and intent of the overall vision was a great match, and Patrick was the perfect client. He is a very hip, modern man. At the time, he was single but wanted a home that would be timeless, with an edge. For a Manhattanite like Patrick, it needed to have that electricity, while also being expandable to eventually accommodate a family."

They incorporated the unexpected throughout the entire house but intensified the edge in the lower level, especially in the lounge area flowing into the wine cave. Imagine an English-style hotel created by a designer who has spent time in New York and North Africa. The effect is clean yet sensual, with urban sophistication. There are colorful flecks of detail, like comfy square poufs covered with Rabat-esque embroidery. McMahon's desire for a rich mix of forms and textures is reflected in the leather sofas. All around the room, circles play off squares. High-voltage gleam from riveted hot rolled steel enrobes the fireplace. The bar area is washed with a glittering mosaic of tile called Honey Onyx Mosaic. Aiello says, "I wanted the light to bounce from the bottles to the onyx to the steel. It's all meant to glow."

Glow indeed. The mosaic glistens like a waterfall shimmering under the full moon. The effect continues into the wine cellar itself, where tiles appear through the glass window on the interior wall of the wine cellar, and covering a column. Aiello brought the hot rolled steel, with its exposed rivets, back for an encore on the wall of the cellar. Zinser, in response, exposed a little bit of the ductwork, "to keep the edge going."

PAGE 38: A hip wine-tasting lounge area, warmed by a fireplace, evokes an English-style hotel via New York and North Africa. There are colorful flecks of detail, such as comfy square poufs covered with Rabat-esque embroidery.

OPPOSITE: McMahon's affinity for a rich mix of forms and textures can be seen in the leather sofas and the play of circles and squares. Riveted hot rolled steel gleams around the fireplace.

But the grounding in wine tradition was left to Zinser. The shelving and cabinetry, from the diamond-shaped bins chosen to break up the visual lines to the display case for McMahon's more important bottles, are made from Zinser's wood of choice, African mahogany. When asked why he is so fond of it, he says, "It's simple. The effect is stunning. I really prefer to incorporate a material that is used for furniture. Mahogany also has balanced tannins, so that over the course of time and exposure to light it doesn't change or darken as drastically as other woods. If the client wants a regal, sophisticated library look, then mahogany is the way to go." But Zinser, whose heart is always "function over form," decided to add a little more to the cellar. "So often," Zinser says, "the

ABOVE: The wine cave that is now stocked with 2,000 bottles wasn't only the client's first wine cellar, but was interior designer Aiello's as well. • "If I had to say what my special bottle was, it would have to be Château Haut-Brion," McMahon says. • Aiello brought the hot rolled steel with its exposed rivets back for an encore on the wall of the cellar.

OPPOSITE: Zinser used African mahogany, the variety of wood he prefers, for the shelves and cabinets in the cellar.

Mahogany plays off stone, which was used extravagantly in the cellar at McMahon's request. He finds the rustic stone has a cool sensuality and that his choice, ivory chiseled wall stone, also lends an air of permanence to the cellar.

material of choice is redwood or cedar—[redwood is not very environmentally sound, and cedar, because of its strong scent, is damaging to the wine]. Importantly, mahogany doesn't have the odor of other oily woods, and keeping those smells out of the wine cellar should be a priority." Zinser also points out that the material is space-warming, and that it takes on greater importance as a counterpoint to steel.

Mahogany also plays off stone, which was used extravagantly in the cellar at McMahon's request. He finds that rustic stone has a cool sensuality and that his choice, the ivory chiseled wall stone, also lends an air of permanence to the cellar.

As befits a world traveler, the cellar is well connected in terms of technology. McMahon can open up the door to the cellar with his fingerprint or from his office in New York or Europe. And one day, he assumes, he'll get around to

putting his inventory on software. But right now, he gets the greatest pleasure from filling his house with guests and family, walking into the cellar, trusting his visual instincts, and plucking what strikes him as right for the moment.

ABOVE: The cellar is well connected in terms of technology. McMahon can access the cellar with his fingerprint or from his office in New York or Europe.

OPPOSITE: "Mahogany doesn't have the odor of other oily woods, and keeping those smells out of the wine cellar should be a priority," says Zinser, who also points out that that the material adds warmth to the space.

CELLAR SNAPSHOT

CAPACITY: 2,000 BOTTLES
CHÂTEAU HAUT-BRION

NARRAGANSETT STYLE

JAMESTOWN, RHODE ISLAND

HOW DO YOU PERSUADE A FLORIDIAN ATTACHED TO HER WATER VIEWS TO MOVE TO SNOWY NEW ENGLAND? Romancing the offer is one way. And in this case Susie Turner's husband offered her a gorgeous view of the Narragansett Bay. To further sweeten the deal, he added, "And the wine cellar of your dreams."

The couple first discovered wine in Las Vegas at the Rio Hotel, where they experimented with the bar's creative wine flights. They followed up on that teaser with classes in their hometown of Tampa. But what really gave them their wine fever were California wine country trips. After the Turners inked their names on about fifteen different mailing lists, the wine fridge Susie gave her husband, Bruce, for their first wedding anniversary in 1998—totally in her own self-interest, she admits—was rendered useless.

When the couple arrived in New England, they built their bayfront 10,000-square-foot home, Greyledge, nicknamed "The Petite Manse," as an homage to the architecture of Sir Edward Lutyens. Taking her husband up on his promise about the wine cellar, Susie hired Fred Tregaskis of New England Wine Cellars. Susie is the force behind the cellar design and the collection. "Bruce really prefers white wine. If 1958 Hanzell Vineyards Pinot is my favorite, his is Kistler Chardonnay," she says. But he's also pretty happy with a good beer."

Regardless of the difference in their tastes, both husband and wife had an investment in seeing that the cellar reflected elements of the Rio Hotel's bar, where they not only first learned about wine but also were married. "There are design components in the bar we wanted in our cellar. We loved the brickwork and the arched ceilings. We wanted the feel of Old World, but because I had these other elements in the house, such as the English oak in the bar right outside of the cellar, we couldn't go too rustic."

Tregaskis received another directive from the couple: Make it lively and avoid the wine store–like grid. As a trained artist, Tregaskis segued into wine cellar–building when he worked in New York, supporting his art by building commercial cellars for such high-profile clients as the Gramercy Tavern. "Now, I look at wine cellars as set design," he explains. "If I had to state my preference it would be for cellars with something off-center, lived in, not perfect."

OVERLEAF: To convince Susie Turner to move, her husband offered her a gorgeous view of Narragansett Bay and the wine cellar of her dreams.

ABOVE: Center stage holds the work area. A table was needed for uncorking and restacking bottles. Framing the table are stubby oak columns. Tregaskis said, "That was the solution to hide some very unseemly steel supports."

OPPOSITE: For their cellar, the Turners wanted an Old World feel to match the English oak in the bar and lounge right outside the cellar.

CELLAR SNAPSHOT

CAPACITY: 2,800 BOTTLES
(COLLECTION 1,000)

HANZELL PINOT 1953

Working toward his audience, as if a curtain would lift to reveal the cellar, he made sure their eyes would dance on the proscenium. The space pulses with redbrick, oak, and redwood, punctuated with high-polish granite, which balances out the room and prevents the overly rustic look Susie feared. The series of brick arches overhead have the slope of a baguette pan. While the room is almost mono-chromatic in reds, the changes in texture give it life. Center stage holds the work area. There had been some discussion of a dining table but Susie insisted to Bruce—who had been lobbying for it—"I'm not eating at fifty-five degrees." A table was needed, but even though it occasion-ally bears a plate of cheese or prosciutto, its main purpose is as a surface for uncorking and restacking bottles. Framing the table are stubby oak columns. Tregaskis says, "That was the solution to hiding some very unseemly steel supports."

The couple wanted to avoid the common home-cellar weakness of looking too much like a wine store. They chose

The space pulses with the redbrick, oak, and redwood punctuated with high-polish granite. The series of brick arches overhead have the slope of a baguette pan.

Dramatic redwood cascades cut
into the space dramatically and
render plucking wine off easy.

scalloped, lacy cubbyholes, one of Susie's favorite features because it is so unusual. She also loves the dramatic redwood cascades; plucking wine off of them is a breeze, and they do exactly as Tregaskis intended—cut into the space dramatically and make the room homey.

That intention arose partly from Susie and Bruce's wish for intimacy in their storage space. In fact, they almost wish the cellar (which holds wine mostly from their mailings, with labels like Peter Michaels, Kistler, Hanzell, Paul Hobbs, and a sprinkling of Australian and Italian) were smaller. "It will hold twenty-eight hundred—but we have over a thousand," Susie explains. "It's very easy for me to lose track of what's there. I haven't gone over to any software system yet." However, she does have some organization, even if it is a bit loose; "I keep the reds on one side and the whites on the other."

The residents of Greyledge view themselves as wine everymen, not connoisseurs. "We're just consumers and have a good time with it. It's fun. And of course we enjoy a good bottle, but we don't have to have a five-hundred-dollar one to think it's worthwhile." When having people over for dinner, the couple always gives their guests a charge by suggesting they go browsing and pick out something they want. There's only one caveat; Susie's favorite Hanzell Pinot 1953 is off-limits. "I only have those on my birthday. And we only have six bottles of it down there! Yesterday I got my yearly allocation: just two. So, if a guest pulls one, I just say well, let's do the *other* Hanzell Pinot."

When they take that uncorked Pinot and wineglasses and walk out directly through the small windowed door, through the bar area, resplendent in gleaming oak flooring, through the sliding doors, and onto the deck with the full-frontal view of Narragansett Bay, it seems as if no one misses Florida at all.

OPPOSITE: Tregaskis received a directive from the couple: Make it lively and avoid the wine store–like grid. They also chose scalloped, lacy cubbyholes, one of Susie's favorite features because it is so unusual.

ABOVE: Just past the cellar, through the sliding doors, is a deck with spectacular views of Narragansett Bay.

ASIAN FLAIR

GRANITE SPRINGS, NEW YORK

THE WIFE OF THE FORMER CEO OF A PROMI-NENT FASHION HOUSE IS A SELF-DESCRIBED CITY GIRL, used to being forty minutes from JFK, ready to jet off to Paris, Milan, or Tokyo. "I went kicking and screaming to this farm in Westchester," she says, laughing.

But he was done with urban life. "I want to have fun now," he says, and for him, that meant being out in the country, near his horses, and with room to entertain, whether at dinners for an intimate group of a hundred or football Sundays spent with friends. Another objective was to have the time and space to carve out a wine collection. "I don't even think of it as collecting, I just think of it as a group of wines I happen to have nearby. What I like to drink is Bordeaux. You know, I used to think it was a lot of hype about French wines being so wonderful. But the more you drink, the more your palate gets attuned to fine wine, and they're great! Margaux is my favorite. The owner, Corinne Mentzelopoulos, invited us once. Now, those cellars are just incredible." Their love of classic (Old World) wines also influenced their vision for their cellar.

The conceptions of the room for the wines started out rough. "I said, Okay, if a cellar is what you want, you find the architect," his wife recalls of her challenge to her husband. He found Rebecca Rasmussen, a Manhattan-based architect, and chose her because of the ease of their rapport. "We talked, and she just got it—and me."

They found another ally in Kelly Hoppen, a London-based designer with an East-meets-West sensibility that spoke to his wife. "Three women working together—that's a little unusual," she says, adding with a laugh, "And still speaking to each other!"

Even though his wife had at first abdicated, she soon became immersed in details of cellar design and added curiosities like the finely woven metal lemon basket she found in an antiques store, and the sconces that throw warm light on the dark wood.

Reclaimed mahogany was the wood of choice for the floors because of its warmth. She wanted to echo that on the doors and on the shelving but the shade had to be the deepest, richest chocolate. "The workers had to strip and re-stain quite a few times until they got it right."

In the end, there wasn't enough room for the wine. "This happens a lot," says cellar designer Fred Tregaskis. "The customer always says, 'Two thousand bottles? That's plenty.' But you know, nature abhors a vacuum. Everybody builds their cellar too small." In this case, the issue was remedied by adding two wings, like in a library, to either side of the main cellar. These add easily accessible room for more bottles, break up the large space, and give it a more intimate, warmer feel.

How to make the room inviting was another challenge. The use of mahogany was just not enough to counterpoint the coldness of the rough-and-tumble poured concrete floors. That's when the layering began. In the tasting room, under the old Japanese writing table, there's a beige, heavy pile rug with Asian accents. In the wine cellar lie not one but two silk-blend rugs, in shades of wheat and toast.

Arched, mahogany-framed glass doors divide the game room (where the pool table lives) from the tasting room. Another pair of doors is set into a glass wall separating the tasting room from the cellar. To add more texture, Rebecca hired a bronze-worker to create a lattice. The heavy burnished metal glows in a moody, sexy way in the sconce "candlelight." "That tasting room is a terrific winter space," the lady of the house says. "And now it's so cozy."

In the cellar itself, bronze makes way for copper. "The goal was not to have everything be the same; the question always was, how to give the room depth and richness," she says. "This theme plays out throughout the house; there's

OVERLEAF: Reclaimed mahogany was chosen for the floors because of its warmth. Echoed on the doors and on the shelving the material had to be the deepest, richest chocolate. "The workers had to strip and restain quite a few times until they got it right," says the owner.

OPPOSITE: There wasn't enough room for the wine, so Tregaskis added two wings, like library standards, to either side of the main cellar. These not only add easily accessible room for more bottles, but they break up the large space, giving it a more intimate, warmer feel.

always something that pops." In the cellar, the visual pop comes from the copper top of the display shelves—one on each of the small end tables that abut the libraryesque wings, and a luxuriously long spread on the expansive back wall. This is where her husband will stand the bottles he's chosen to bring upstairs for dinner, or where he'll open one to enjoy with friends over a game of pool.

As for filling the cellar's shelves, that's not her department. "Me? I'm a cheap date," she says, laughing. "Well, not really—I like good wine. My husband knows now what I like." He, on the other hand, takes great joy in thinking about wine. His favorite thing about the cellar is simply that he has one. "I enjoy going down there, even if it's only for

OPPOSITE CLOCKWISE FROM TOP LEFT: The tasting room also houses a small library and reading area. • The homeowner found sconces that throw warm light on the dark wood. • "I don't even think of it as collecting, I just think of it as a group of wines I happen to have nearby," the homeowner says. • A vase holds used corks rather than bouquets.

ABOVE LEFT TO RIGHT: A finely woven metal lemon basket was found in an antique store. • In the cellar, the visual pop comes from the copper top of the display shelves—one on each of the small end tables that abut the library standards • Even the empty bottles add a sense of richness and texture to the cellar.

one bottle for dinner," he says. "I like taking my time, looking at all the labels, thinking about the wine. I like it even more when we have friends over and we go down together to select a wine. Everyone always has something to say."

For her, the best part is the social aspect, the conversation that flows when wine is around. "I love to sit on the sofa, looking out with the doors of the cellar open, and being able to observe, especially with people around, doing their tasting." She adds, with a wink, "You know, my husband is very opinionated."

That may be true, but he also knows what his strengths are and sticks to them. "It's just like it was in my business, and in my whole life," he says, looking over at his wife. "I wasn't in charge of aesthetics. She was."

ABOVE LEFT: Arched, mahogany-framed glass doors divide the games room (where the pool table lives) from the tasting room.

ABOVE RIGHT: The tasting room is an exercise in layering, with an old Japanese writing table on top of a heavy pile rug with Asian accents.

OPPOSITE: The entire entertaining complex allows the owners to always observe their guests. Relaxing on the sofas, they can watch a game of pool or a tasting.

CELLAR SNAPSHOT

CAPACITY: 2,000
CHÂTEAU MARGAUX 1989; 1999
LA MISSION HAUT-BRION, 1990
SUPER TUSCANS: SASSICAIA, 1985

DESIGNED FOR LIVING

BEL AIR, CALIFORNIA

AS AN ENTERTAINMENT LAWYER IN THE LOS ANGELES AREA, Ken Ziffren has had plenty of opportunities to do some entertaining of his own. For the past thirty years his wine collection has served as the centerpiece for the gatherings. He entered the wine world as a lark, playing sidekick to a wine-mad friend, never believing it would lead him down a vinous path. Back in the 1970s, the two would pal around on the weekends, frequenting stores and wineries, tasting and buying. But the pivotal moment occurred after closing a business deal. Celebratory bottles followed: 1961 Lafite and '64 Latour. "At that point, while I knew I didn't want to own a vineyard, I sure wanted to have a good collection of wine to drink."

That happened in short order. First he began investing in Bordeaux. Ziffren then segued to Burgundy, but became disenchanted with what he considered their unreliability. For example, he remembers sitting down to dinner with his wife, looking forward to what should have been a spectacular bottle, the 1990 Comte Georges De Vogüé Chambolle-Musigny. "My wife has a finer palate than I do. She is much quicker to discern whether a wine is good or not. She took one sip and said, 'No, no, no.' I agreed and retrieved another bottle, and the same thing happened! Two more bottles, and we were still not happy." These days he finds more enjoyment with Oregon Pinots and Napa Cabernets. Firm in his insistence that he has never been after extravagant quantities, Ziffren asserts that he is a drinker first, collector second. Accordingly, he takes his physical cellar seriously. The same friend who took him wine tasting was the one who advised him to build his wines a proper home. To date, this experienced cellar owner has had four, running the gamut from a closet to a series of rooms. The one installed in the living room of his 1920s cottage in Bel Air is his emotional favorite.

It never occurred to Ziffren to actually install his 1,200 bottles in the living room. In fact, it seemed counterintuitive; a cellar should be in the cellar. "When we bought the house, one of the big questions was where to put the wine. While we were on a planning tour with our designer we walked into the basement, full of pipes. It was just wrong. There was no way we could get any kind of a decent section for wine. But then we walked into the living room, and I said, could we do something here? And he said, you know, maybe we can. When I

OVERLEAF: Cellar designer Benoit suggested that Ziffren install his 1,200 bottles in the living room.

ABOVE: The two flanking armoires hold 350 bottles each. A mass of venting and wires governs the temperature behind the insulated glass.

CELLAR SNAPSHOT

CAPACITY: 1,500 BOTTLES

1982 MOUTON ROTHSCHILD

1931 QUINTA DO NOVAL

CALIFORNIA CABERNETS:
ABREU

BLANKIET

COLGIN

FRANK FAMILY

HOURGLASS

SCARECROW

SEAVEY

SHAFER HILLSIDE SELECT

saw Ben Benoit's drawings for three different wine armoires, built into walls, I really flipped."

The result was a trio of dark wood alcoves and their contents framing the room. Scattered empty bottles of sentimental value dot the windowsills. The decanters and the bone-handled corkscrews reinforce the wine theme. This is a cellar for the classicist who loves clean lines. The largest wine alcove that presides over the room holds 800 bottles; the two flanking ones hold 350 bottles each. They look so spare; it's hard to comprehend the mass of venting and wires that governs the temperature behind the insulated glass. The choice to place the wines in the living room ended up being an inspired one, because the room is perched directly on top of the basement. Concerned about keeping the wines cool and the room silent, the Ziffrens didn't want any buzz from the air-conditioning unit. Because of the basement's proximity, Benoit easily created an out-of-sight, vented commercial duct system. Not only was it easy; it also made for a whisper-soft air-control system.

The trio of dark wood alcoves and their contents frame the room.

The one unfortunate part of the project was that it had to sacrifice some of the home's original detail. Benoit needed an additional two feet of depth in each wall to afford the space for each of the cellar alcoves. Benoit explained, "The house was built in 1928, and the crown moldings were built by Italian craftsmen who specialized in plaster. It killed us to do it—the moldings had to be demolished. But because this is also an historic house, they needed to be somehow reinstalled. The molds for them no longer exist; consequently, we had to duplicate them in wood."

Benoit sought to achieve an organic flow from the comfortable cottage furniture to the elegant millwork of the cellars, and the Ziffrens love it. "We've had no problems with

OPPOSITE CLOCKWISE FROM TOP LEFT: Precious vintages—with low-tech tags—can easily be pulled from the wine armoires. • The decanters and the bone-handled corkscrews reinforce the wine message. • Ziffren also collects corks of sentimental value.

ABOVE: Being surrounded by wine storage in a comfortable room gives new meaning to the expression "meditation wine."

the cellar at all," Ken Ziffren says. "Even the times our power went out, the generator kicked in. It's quiet and I also love its location. In the past my cellars were out of the way, around the corner, down the steps, far away from the action. There was plenty to deal with before a corkscrew was ever drawn and a cork pulled."

He finds that having a comfortable room in the center of his wine storage gives a whole new meaning to the term "meditation wine." "We've got a fantastic view of the garden. It's a great place to contemplate what to open. You know, I don't think we would ever have used the room so much if the wines were elsewhere. Then this would have been solely a guest-entertaining room, the formal room. But now it's our refuge. Ellen and I find ourselves coming here whether we're with people or by ourselves. We escape here. There's no TV and no phone. Just us. And it's a great place to connect." After all, when you are surrounded by 1,200 magnums and bottles of old Bordeaux and young Cabernets, who needs distraction?

ABOVE LEFT: In order to accommodate the space for the alcoves, the moldings had to be demolished, but Benoit re-created them in wood.

ABOVE RIGHT: Ziffren's favorite cellar is the one he built for this 1920s cottage in Bel Air.

OPPOSITE: The Ziffrens line the windowsills with empty bottles of sentimental value.

PART II

THE GENTLEMAN'S HAVEN

These cellars belong to the Connoisseurs. The owners of these boys' clubs celebrate their garages stocked with Aston Martin DB9s just as they do their rooms stacked with precious wines. Built for extensive wine collections, these cellars are overflowing with fantastic Old World examples. Classic in style, their storage spaces are composed of elegant wood racks and timeless materials, such as rugged stone, limestone, and copper. But their classical aesthetics can be deceiving. These cellars also feature innovative layouts and racking systems that ensure any collection has sufficient room to grow.

For most serious collectors, one collection isn't enough. The oenophiles featured here have collections within collections, and cellars within a cellar. Special storage solutions have been designed to accommodate monumental collections; some hit the 60,000 bottle mark. For such spaces, there are double racking systems and separate wings designated for the reds and for the whites. Every inch counts.

As collections are personal, emotional endeavors, these cellars often manifest the results of decades of pursuing the perfect bottle. Accordingly, these men have created havens that frame their journeys from their first bottles to their latest acquisitions.

THE ROYAL TREATMENT

ARMONK, NEW YORK

FOR YEARS TOM STRAUSS, THE CEO AND FOUNDING PARTNER OF A PROMINENT INVESTMENT-BANKING FIRM, had to make do with slapdash wine storage and its dark side: chaos. A familiar scene: Dinner guests are about to arrive while the proud owner of the sixty-thousand-bottle collection bends over and tugs at multiple boxes. He mutters to himself, "Damn it, where are those 1986 Margaux?"

How could one blame him? While this is an otherwise extremely orderly man, wooden crates were scattered about in almost every room of the eighteenth-century farmhouse and the Park Avenue residence he shares with his wife, Bonnie. It was in this way, Strauss quips, that he "intimidated my wife into the wine cellar." After all, one can go for just so long with wine bottles underfoot.

The journey started in the early '90s, when his then-fellow partner at Salomon Brothers collared him to join a friendly wine-buying club. "The partner was to make all of the choices for the four of us. All I know is that the bill came every month and so did the cases." In a very short time his collection expanded. The crates multiplied. Luckily, the wine-happy colleague had

excellent taste and liked to buy in quantities, which is how Strauss happens to still have twenty cases of 1986 Margaux. "Given the vintages that were available then, mid- to late '80s and early '90s, the foundation for my wine collection was mostly French and mostly Bordeaux."

When the buying quartet stopped, Strauss had to fend for himself. He started to make his own decisions and branched out to add Super Tuscans and Californians into the mix. Before he could say "renovate," he had five thousand cases literally underfoot. The aberrant boxes made the wine cellar an absolute necessity, and the need for a wine cellar was the driving excuse behind the house renovation.

The couple's plank farmhouse perches on the top of a hill on the cusp between Connecticut and New York. Nestled in the middle of several acres of landscaped and wooded greenery, it is sequestered at a distance from the road, surrounded by gentle nature. With one hill excavation, the wine cellar project, headed by a stellar team, was on its way.

Architect Elliott Rosenblum explains that the wine experience begins with the staircase leading downstairs and with the expanse of glass doors that washes the

whole lower level in natural light. At the bottom is a take on a modern-day entertainment center: wet bar, gym, billiard room, and not one cellar but two. To the left are floor-to-ceiling showroom-like glass panes through which one can view the entrance to the very adult wine cellar. Behind the staircase, above folding louvered doors, hangs a rustic, rough-hewn sign that Strauss had made out in the Hamptons; it reads CHILDREN'S WINE CAVE—a small area for guests and his grown kids to select wines.

For the adult cellar, large storage spaces and a full wine experience were on tap. Strauss was extremely hands-on during the process and prepared a roster of requirements to

hand off to Rosenblum and designers Elissa Cullman, Heidi Kravis, and David Spon. On top of his wish list was an adjacent tasting room that would be large enough in which to entertain pre- and post-dinner. The space also needed to be cigar-friendly with proper ventilation. "My wife is anti-smoking," he explains. "So we had to make sure the smell didn't linger." The ambience he sought in his tasting room was Old English antique wood; for the cellar, terra-cotta and Old Europe.

The floor-to-ceiling window wall separating the real world from the wine experience allows natural light in the tasting room, which ended up being a spacious square with

OVERLEAF: Strauss's cellar called for large storage spaces and a full wine experience. He was extremely hands-on during the process.

ABOVE: Tom Strauss and his wife, Bonnie. • One of Strauss's foremost wishes was to have an adjacent tasting room with an old English antique feeling.

OPPOSITE: A thousand-liter barrel whose head is embedded in the stone wall was purchased complete through a local antiques company. • The client also collects wine paraphernalia. Decking out the sideboard are stunning antique decanters and candlesticks. • Rosenblum created a European-style cellar with a serpentine sensibility. • The tasting room is also adorned with elegant English funnels.

ten-foot ceilings. It appears to be surrounded by rustic stone walls, which are actually, as Rosenblum says, "Beautifully appointed stone that passes as structural, instead of what it really is, veneer. I took inspiration from those great old stone walls all around that part of Connecticut." The stone is hand-tooled and hand-picked. The hardware is likewise antique. The doors appear to be all hand-pegged, and the wide antique oak floorboards give a very intense handcrafted atmosphere.

Rosenblum, listening to the request for a more authentic European cellar instead of a straightforward big box, created one with the serpentine appeal of an old cellar in Burgundy—without the mold-covered bottles, that is. Walking through the space's zigzag, one feels a sense of adventure. Spon installed plenty of custom-made nooks and crannies, perfect for those multiple crates, individual bottles, and oversized magnums and double mags.

Strauss, who has the collecting gene in more ways than wine, found most of the appointments. Not only is he crazy about old flags and Americana, but also about wine paraphernalia. Examples abound in the tasting room. Decking out the sideboard are stunning antique decanters, elegant English funnels, too many corkscrews, and an abundance of teardrop stemware, to which he is especially drawn because each one is a one-off. He said unapologetically, "You have to be obsessive. It comes with the territory." That is the only explanation for the thousand-liter barrel, the head of which is embedded into the stone wall. He purchased the complete barrel through a local antiques company, "But when I bought it, I knew I was going to dismantle it and only use the head. It was bought in and shipped from France with enormous aggravation and expense."

ABOVE: The cellar's rustic stone walls are actually appointed stone that passes as structural instead of what it really is: veneer. They were inspired by great old stone walls common in that part of Connecticut. The stone is hand tooled and hand picked.

OPPOSITE LEFT TO RIGHT: Sometimes when an evening kicks off with pre-dinner cocktails and cheese in the tasting room, guests forgo the dining room. • Strauss happens to still have twenty cases of 1986 Margaux. "Given the vintages that were available then, mid- to late eighties and early nineties, the foundation for my wine was mostly French and mostly Bordeaux." • The Champagnes, the Burgundies, and his Bordeaux, each have their own places in the cellar.

Guests are reluctant to leave the room, he has discovered. On frequent occasions, when an evening kicks off with pre-dinner cocktails, they just never make it to the dining room. How could they be blamed when faced with the pièce de résistance?

While there is a general logic to how Strauss organizes his bottles, it is approximate. The Champagnes, for his wife, the Burgundies, and the jewel of the collection, his Bordeaux, each have their own places. And along with obscene amounts of old Bordeaux there are plenty of other gems, including the assortment of Domaine de la Romanée-Conti, and some eccentricities such as older Mas de Daumas Gassac.

After pulling a wine from his Bordeaux section, Grand Vin de Leoville, 1985, Strauss puts his nose into the bowl of a Schott Zwiesel glass and says, "The day I moved my wine into the cellar was an emotional one. When the wine arrived, I was here," Strauss continues, getting energized by the memory. He takes a sip (it's profound, soapy with some sweet potato and loads of personality). "There is absolutely nothing like a great Bordeaux, is there?"

CELLAR SNAPSHOT

CAPACITY: 60,000 BOTTLES
1986 MARGAUX
DOMAINE DE LA ROMANÉE-CONTI
MAS DE DAUMAS GASSAC
GRAND VIN DE LEOVILLE, 1985

THE CHILDREN'S CELLAR

The inspiration for this petite cellar came about one fateful night when Strauss's married son and friends became thirsty and raided Daddy's wine cellar. "It turns out my son didn't know the difference between bar wine and good wine, so he got into the older White Burgundies, Cortons, and Montrachets," Strauss said with a grimace. "I don't begrudge him anything in the world, but to drink those without appreciating them!"

New England–based David Spon was in charge of wine-cellar shelving construction and design. In Spon's work he hears versions of that story—*So-and-so got into my collection and you won't believe what they drank!*— all the time. His favorite is the one about a client, the owner of an investment firm, who returned home after a hard day, opened the fridge, and found one-third left in a bottle of 1978 Guigal La Landonne. He was mystified. He was irate. He was . . . homicidal. He was going to blame one of his kids. When the cook was interrogated, the client found out that the bottle, one carried carefully home from a recent auction, had been used in Monday's meat loaf.

Spon's fix for that particular persnickety problem was a few of those diamond-shaped cubbyholes that hold nine bottles that can be fair game for houseguest or meat loaf. But given how this current client wanted his son and daughter to feel cared for, he made the decision to build them a cellar of their own. The shelves hold about 150 bottles and get fed with wines regularly by Strauss—reliable Bordeaux like Lynch-Bages, Oregon Pinots like Yamhill, and a smattering of international whites. "Believe me," he says, "they're well taken care of."

WINE IN HIS BLOOD

WESTHAMPTON, NEW YORK

GROWING UP IN GERMANY, SVEN BORHO HAD INTIMATE KNOWLEDGE OF GRAPES long before he decided to drink them. When he was old enough to hold a secateur, this energetic European investment banker worked the harvest for his grandparents' vineyards. "We all did," Sven Borho explains. "When the grapes come in, you don't have a choice. It's like a birth. You roll up your sleeves, grab a clipper, and get to work."

Home for him was in the southern part of Germany, on the Rhine in Durbach, a town known for Riesling, a bit of light-bodied Pinot Noir, and Eiswein, the much-sought-after sweet wine made from grapes frozen on the vine in the deep of winter.

"Isn't it ironic that I wasn't a big wine fan at all until I moved to the States?" Sven muses. "I initially got intrigued when I started going to the Hamptons and had French friends who introduced me to Bordeaux. Another friend, who was the sommelier at the restaurant Jean-Georges, took me in hand, and that was what really helped me to develop my palate." Borho soon came full circle, and rediscovered his German roots. Accordingly, when the opportunity came along to buy

some of the family's lost vineyards at auction, he made sure he was not outbid. "I rent the vines out to local wine-makers. It is very gratifying to have that connection reinstated," he said.

Stocking mostly French and German wines, Borho originally started to store them in one portable wine cooler, then graduated to two. In 2003 he bought his current weekend home, a converted historic 1880 hotel, with a sweeping staircase inside and a carpet of lawn that stretches to the water. The idea of the dream wine cellar started to seep into his consciousness. It took him a few years to get to work on it, however. First, Borho wanted to move in and live there for a while, get the feel of his new home, and begin to intuit where he wanted to install it.

One day while sitting by the fire in his living room, Borho found the location he was looking for. "The living room is one of my favorite spaces, yet it was underutilized. I wanted to give it purpose. I wanted a reason to bring people there. A wine cellar was just the thing. I could envision the image from the living room. I wanted something very handsome."

His plan was to gather friends by the fire, where they would alternate between staring at the embers and gazing through a sheer glass pane at his more than 3,500 bottles. Once in the right mood, he'd dispatch a friend to decide which bottle would be their next. However, the one problem with this fantasy was the reality that there was no other room attached to the living room. Further complicating his original idea was that on the other side of the wall was the outdoors. So demolition of a standing wall was required and the living room area needed to be built out. Borho chose cellar designer Lee Zinser as his man. The client, who knows his own tendencies to be exacting, says he was a little concerned that "I was going to drive him nuts."

Far from it. Zinser loves clients who know what they want. He also loves using materials that have a story, and in this case, he explains, "Everything in the cellar has some story to tell. From the two-thousand-year-old Jerusalem stone underfoot to the light fixtures above, it all has a purpose and reason. I particularly like those lights. Because of the connection the house has to the sea, we thought these reclaimed bell-shaped searchlights off of an early 1900s ship worked really well. They also have the feel of a corkscrew."

Luminescent, with its monochromatic earth tones of ochre and orange, the space is also smallish at 16 feet wide by 20 feet deep. This is a solid wine room, built to last and very masculine. The point was to trick the brain into believing the structure had permanence. Pains were taken to this end, such as incorporating plenty of stone and brick

OVERLEAF: The 16-feet-wide by 20-feet-deep cellar is warm and luxurious with walls that glow in earth tones, and a floor made of two-thousand-year-old Jerusalem limestone adds to the lushness of the space.

RIGHT: The koa wood, which comprises the cellar's racks, complements the mahogany and other red tones in the rest of the house.

OPPOSITE: The salvaged, bell-shaped searchlights from an early 1900s ship look like corkscrews.

columns and arches. Borho particularly wanted an arch made from the same color brick used in the outdoor gate, the house entryway, and his Japanese garden, to create that continuity. This seamless design was important to both client and designer.

Then there is the wood; warm, rare, and as polished as a piano. "I love exotic woods," Borho explains. He set his cap for koa, the wood most familiar from the backs of violins. "The house has lots of different kinds of mahoganies and teaks, and this was another layer to bring in. I like the color variation in the wood, and there was another reason. I am three hundred feet from the water. Lee and I were very worried about getting flooded, which, by the way, was one

reason not to put the cellar underground. Many canoes are made from koa; we knew it was water-worthy, if it needed to be tested." Then he laughs. "Who am I kidding? Of course all of that is true, but it is still a rationalization because the reason I chose the wood is because I loved the way it would provide counterpoint for the mahogany in the house and play with the assortment of red colors. That wood in this kind of quantity is so hard to get hold of. In the end, I was difficult, you see; I probably drove Lee crazy in other ways too."

But Zinser insists it wasn't the case, even when Borho wanted a certain storage system Zinser really doesn't recommend, diamond bins. He explains that diamond bins can be a disaster—while they offer efficient storage, their layered

ABOVE LEFT: The cellar's arch is comprised of the same color brick as the outdoor gate, entryway, and Japanese garden.

ABOVE RIGHT: The aboveground cellar is just three hundred feet from the ocean and is made from the same kind of wood as canoes. Says Borho, "We knew it was water-worthy."

TECHNOLOGY AND
THE WINE CELLAR

Today's wine cellars use all kinds of toys for girls and (especially) boys to organize collections, control the climate, and allow for remote access.

For example, to transform a room filled with wine bottles into a cellar with a world-class data-management system, Peter Kend called Marc Lazar of Cellar Advisers, LLC. A consulting company for wine lovers, Cellar Advisers works with designers and software companies to build infrastructures that help collectors manage and maintain their collections. Lazar did for Kend what he does for the majority of his clients: He installed Cellar Tracker, a user-created, online database that monitors the comings and goings of every bottle in the cellar. Cellar Tracker offers users a number of additional perks, including a constant stream of real tasting notes by real collectors; automatic appraisals of your collection based on current auction prices; and, "over drinking age" alerts, so you know which wines to drink right away. Clients like Kend, who are long on bottles and short on time, hire Lazar and his team to input the bottles into the system. When a bottle is finished, the client swipes the label and Cellar Tracker, using a bar-code system, takes note. Lazar also advises cellar owners to consider installing environmental monitoring systems with sensors that wirelessly track the conditions in a cellar; these Internet-based systems promise collectors peace of mind and allow them to access the information from any wireless device, anywhere in the world. Best of all, Lazar helps clients put these comprehensive databases into appealing packages: There's not a wire in sight (they are tucked away behind drawers and panels) and the sleek monitor by Apple, which is integrated seamlessly on a display wall, plays a continual slideshow of the most beautiful vineyards in the world.

Lee Zinser of Cellar Works also employs advanced technology in his cellars. For his jet-setting clients he installs special locks that open cellar doors with the owner's fingerprint. Linked with Crestron, collectors can open the door remotely from anywhere there is computer access.

Climate controls are often the most important element for a cellar, and to address condensation issues Zinser uses M Prestige Clear Film on glass windows, which prevents ultraviolet light from damaging the wine. The absence of metal in these new films prevents corrosion on the film and does not interfere with wireless and cellular signals.

Regardless of the extent of the technology and whatever gadgets the collector might have, the visitors always notice the wine the most.

nature also makes bottle breakage more likely. "In the old days," he says, "when there were two shapes of bottles—Burgundy and Bordeaux shapes—the bins were adequate. But today there are so many different bottle shapes that stacking them in the bins can be difficult." Nevertheless, Zinser receives plenty of requests for them, especially when the cellar has a full frontal view, like this one. "The one thing they do well is to break up the line. They're easy on the eye."

And Borho did want to show off his cellar, after all. So at first they thought they would put the room on display through a large window. Then that idea changed to a glass door. At last the idea morphed into a glass wall. Done. To solve a problem they had with condensation, they used a new product from the 3M company, M Prestige Clear Film, which also prevents ultraviolet light from damaging the wine. More problems arose when the sliding door needed a steel

frame, but the metal didn't fit the house's aesthetic. An artisan who could paint the frame to look like wood was found. The cellar also has the full complement of technology: fingerprint control and a Crestron system, which allows remote access to the cellar. "If Sven wants to open the door for deliveries while he's on business in Europe, that is all possible," Zinser says.

"All of these little details," Borho says, "added plenty of work for Lee. But it was exciting. The process was so alive that unlike what most people experience during construction—hell, the journey was almost as good as the end result."

CELLAR SNAPSHOT

CAPACITY: 3,500 BOTTLES
BORDEAUX, RIESLING, AND PORT

OPPOSITE: To show off his 3,500-bottle collection, Borho installed a glass wall instead of a mere window.

ABOVE: Borho integrated his cellar with his fireplace, recreation area, and media room, giving guests adequate eye candy. • Borho displays his collections of glasses, whiskeys, and other liquor in a custom-made koa breakfront in the center of the cellar.

THE NATURAL

YOUNTVILLE, CALIFORNIA

FLEEING BUDAPEST AFTER THE 1956 REVOLUTION, LOU KAPCSÁNDY LANDED IN CALIFORNIA and quickly became a professional football player for the San Diego Chargers. His fortune, however, was made not in sports but as the head of a large general-contracting company in Seattle. After his retirement Kapcsándy wanted to return to California, and hunted around Napa for his next act. The choice was a natural: He had romanced his wife, Bobbie, there decades before, and when the couple found the historic State Lane Vineyard, they couldn't resist; they surprised themselves by turning Kapcsándy's hobby into a wine-making and wine-importing business.

Wine had been a fixture for Kapcsándy since his initial purchase of the 1961 St. Julien, Château Leoville Lascasse. After his first taste of that wine, which he had upon its release in 1964, he didn't have to be convinced of wine's importance. "You know," he says, "I'm not a collector, I just overbuy!" What he does buy are wines that are generally drinkable on release but will greatly improve down the road. More recently he has been forgoing out-of-the-gate vintages in favor of private collections in liquidation.

Kapcsándy's first "cellar" consisted of boxes stashed under a staircase. The next was a petite 100 square feet. A 400-square-foot storage space with off-the-rack racking followed, but it was still extremely inadequate for twenty-eight thousand bottles, and most of his collection had to be stored in commercial rental spaces. Now, with American and Hungarian flags flying together like doves outside of the Kapcsándy Family Winery, he has pooled all his bottles under one roof in his Napa-inspired home, thanks to Patrick Wallen of Artistic Wine Cellars.

Kapcsándy was ready to sign off on the plans for a cellar drawn up by a different builder when Wallen, who had been tipped off by a mutual friend that he might still have a chance at the job, stopped by on a cold call. The two found common ground. "I hate to knock someone else's ideas, but when I looked at the drawings, I saw that he wasn't being given a whole lot of room to move in there. I thought he could do better.

"Lou had already pared his cellar down to twenty thousand bottles, but it was still a hell of a lot of inventory to shoehorn into eight hundred square feet. Double the footage would have been my ideal. He also didn't

OVERLEAF: Kapcsándy's 20,000 bottles are stored in only 800 square feet. "Double the footage would have been my ideal," says his designer.

ABOVE LEFT: "My sister is an artist. She was visiting from Hungary. I woke up one night at three a.m. and there she was on the pulpit stool, painting. It was a terrific gift," says Kapcsándy.

ABOVE RIGHT: The Kapcsándy coat of arms floats above the door to the cellar, just off the combined living/dining room.

OPPOSITE: Bottles are stacked up to ten feet high with peninsulas comprised of larger formats lying horizontally to display the labels.

want anything too flashy," Wallen remembers. Who needs flash with that many bottles? Such abundance is impressive all by itself.

The cellar is off the dining room, through the door earmarked by the Kapcsándy coat of arms, framed by a meticulously hand-painted arbor of grapevines. "My sister is an artist. She was visiting from Hungary. I woke up one night at three a.m. and there she was on the pulpit stool, painting. It was a terrific gift."

Once through the grapevined passage, in the 55-degree coolness, there is an assault of redwood racking, chosen for its indigenousness as well as its resistance to humidity. Bottles, bottles are everywhere—stacked up to ten feet high, with peninsulas sticking out, capped off with plenty of 5- to 8-liter bottles lying horizontally to show off the labels. The collective visual is so breathtaking it's impossible not to reflexively reach for a corkscrew.

Kapcsándy still favors Bordeaux, which comprise 60 percent of his inventory, but lest one thinks he's forgotten

his now-hometown of Napa, wooden crates branded with names like Screaming Eagle, Opus One, and Caymus testify otherwise. Toward the rear of the cellar, the intensity and density of bottles ramps up. Overhead, pergolas and arches are packed with bottles, all accentuating the spirit of vinous cornucopia. "Engineering those wooden bottle arches was difficult. They weren't always so sturdy!" Wallen admits about the wine-imbedded arches. "They started to swing before one bottle was installed, so I had to rethink the anchoring. I secured them with steel rods in the floor and into the ceiling."

Wallen prefers low-voltage lights, kept close to the racks so they spray the light down. "We typically like to see a dark paint, satin or eggshell, no flat, no semi-gloss, because we want the walls and ceilings to disappear and the focus to be

OPPOSITE CLOCKWISE FROM TOP LEFT: As a nod to his Hungarian roots, Kapcsándy includes kitschy elements in his cellar to add a touch of humor. • Bottles are tucked away in high and very low places. Sometimes Kapcsándy enlists his son to retrieve bottles located in tricky-to-reach locations. • Kapcsándy has a collection of rare ports, some dating back to the early 1800s. • "[The owner] also didn't want anything too flashy," says cellar designer Wallen. "Who needs flash with that many bottles? Such abundance is impressive all by itself."

ABOVE: Kapcsándy still favors Bordeaux, which makes up 60 percent of his collection.

on the racks. I also angled the lighting high to reveal bottle displays at 15 degrees. That way Lou can see every bottle he has, even though I had to double-rack the bottles, which I don't like." At times Kapcsándy must dig into nooks and Hobbit-size holes to get at the wines. More challenging is climbing up on the pulpit stool to get to the top of the 10-foot ceiling to retrieve bottles. "I try to avoid that," says Kapcsándy. "If my son is around, which is often, I put him on the job."

To choose bottles, he and his son sometimes just cruise the space for wine-selection inspiration. At other times they peruse the 212-page inventory list, which luckily comes with a map so they can easily find the desired bottle.

During the process, Wallen had to push the down-to-earth Kapcsándy toward a little more form and function. "Lou had gone so long without the proper cellar conve-

niences he needed to be reminded what was possible. For example, he hadn't considered the benefit of having a countertop where he could unpack, sit some cases, and just look over the wines. And he needed a drawer. Both of those needs were met by fashioning a used oak barrel into a piece for storage inside and a countertop and stool for notes. This is a well-used spot. And while Lou wanted to go with low-wattage flash, I had to talk him into some style, like a special grape-leaf-and-vine motif inlay countertop."

The one element Kapcsándy insisted on was a room within a room, a special place for his most special three thousand bottles, so intent was he on his objective to suspend their aging process. To achieve this in the 55-degree cellar he embedded an additional 45–48-degree cellar, cool enough to throw the old gems into dormancy, into the left side of his cellar. Within it rest beauties like pre-Communist

ABOVE: A special room stores 3,000 rare and mature bottles and suspends their aging process.

Tokai and Bordeaux from the early 1900s. "My son went in there on Father's Day and pulled a 1918. That's what it's there for. To drink, not to look at. The truth was, it was maderized, not enjoyable. So we pulled a 1937 Hospices de Beaune Volnay Cuvée Blondeau from Camille Giroud. What a gorgeous wine!"

While Kapcsándy is indeed a man drawn to function, one of his favorite elements ended up being his floor. "It's poured concrete, a combo of stencils right on it with subtle grape leaves and veins etched on top. Its brilliance is that it is very clean, doesn't stain, and is easy to mop."

And so with vines on the floor, counters, and in racks all around him, Kapcsándy envelops his guests with his ever-growing passion.

ABOVE LEFT: The Kapcsándy family crest adorns a crate from the owner's homeland.

ABOVE CENTER: The bottles are most dense at the rear of the cellar where, overhead, pergolas and arches are filled with bottles. "Engineering those wooden bottle arches was difficult. They weren't always so sturdy!" Wallen admitted.

ABOVE RIGHT: At times, Kapcsándy must dig into nooks and Hobbit-size holes to reach the wines.

CELLAR SNAPSHOT

CAPACITY: 20,000 BOTTLES
1980 BERINGER
1874 CHÂTEAU LAFITE ROTHSCHILD
1905 CHÂTEAUX MARGAUX
1943 VOLNAY
1955 PETRUS
1830 MADEIRAS

WOODEN WONDERLAND

WOODSIDE, CALIFORNIA

THE KEECHES DON'T STAND ON CEREMONY; IN THEIR WOODSIDE, CALIFORNIA, household they choose not to hold on to special bottles for special occasions. "There's not a bottle in there I wouldn't drink," Max Keech says of his 1,300-bottle cellar. "I buy what I like and what my wife likes, bottles we think taste good and are interesting."

Keech, the head of Keech Properties, L.L.C., a Bay Area real-estate corporation specializing in sustainable and environmentally sensitive development, has an inside line on "interesting" too: A good friend of his owns CrauforD, an exclusive, small-production winery in Napa, and tips him off to up-and-coming names and particularly good bottlings. That's how he found Hourglass and Gemstone from Napa, and, most recently, Ghost Block from Oakville. "The first Cab release—the 2004—was a big, well rounded, wonderful wine," he says. "They just released the 2005—I can't wait to try it after it gets four to six more months in the cellar."

Keech wasn't able to have the luxury of waiting that long back when he stored wines in wooden crates in the closet, or even when he upgraded to a sixty-bottle under-counter cooler. But as soon as he saw this house, the real-estate developer side of him kicked in and he began imagining the wine cellar it could hold. "It's a large house with an unfinished basement," he explains. "It seemed like an ideal space in which to create an entertainment center for ourselves and our kids, and to be able to entertain friends."

Entertaining is a big part of the Keech lifestyle. As Tom Warner, his cellar designer, says, "This home is all about easy California living." Dinners are often held outside, cooked in an outdoor kitchen surrounded by the Pinot Noir vines the Keeches planted a couple of years ago—vines that may well supply them with their own label of wine one day. The 1,500-acre Wunderlich County Park lies just beyond, giving the space an exclusive yet expansive feeling.

After an evening on the patio, guests head to the basement, a cool oasis of limestone tile with warm wood accents. The centerpiece of the space is an eight-foot billiards table topped with rich Tuscan-yellow felt that matches the hue of the plaster walls. Four swivel-top stools with playful billiard-ball-patterned cushions provide a place to perch between turns and drink some wine.

The 8-foot billiards table with yellow felt matches the hue of the plaster walls.

The wine cellar is a long, warmly lit room of distressed wood and limestone tile flooring with wood accents in yellow and cocoa tones.

Visible from the table, the wine cellar is a long, warmly lit room of distressed wood on the other side of the walnut-framed glass door. "It was a natural fit off the billiard room," Keech says. "We can take out a bottle and taste it while banging around a few balls." They'll open that bottle— starting the evening, perhaps, with a favorite Pinot Noir like Williams Selyem, Pisoni, or Sea Smoke—at the billiard-room bar, whose countertop is an impressive slab of Brazilian chocolate, twister granite. When Keech needs another bottle, he grasps the heavy, handsome iron door handle and pulls it open, and guests follow, seduced by the warm glow emanating from the cellar.

The warm yellow and cocoa tones continue inside. This was one of the very first cellars Warner ever designed using distressed reclaimed walnut instead of the more common redwood. "For walnut, the challenge is getting enough good

material, free of knots," he points out. "Walnut is also a much harder wood, and therefore trickier to work with, and it is also very easy to make it look like plastic, something that must be avoided," Warner says. "Working with the wood stain is like working with makeup; you can either put it on so it's obvious or so that it's hardly noticeable."

There's no mistaking these shelves for plastic. The technique Warner developed to distress and stain the wood created a burnished bourbon hue a few shades darker than the golden floor and ceiling. This gives the wood a softness and creates an impression that the shelves are cradling the wines, coddling them in a bath of warm indirect light. Tiny LEDs on the double row of angled displays draw extra attention to favored treasures.

Keech had done a lot of research before designing the cellar—"I'm a bit of an open-house junkie," he admits—and

PAGE 100: Says designer Warner about the three mirror-backed arches that serve as display spaces, "They add depth—really important in a long, narrow space like this. You get this sense of an infinity of wine bottles."

ABOVE LEFT TO RIGHT: The arches did cost Keech space for more wine, but as Keech says, "It's a 1,300-bottle cellar—I knew I wasn't going to go above that number. • The cellar entry is a walnut framed glass door with a heavy, handsome iron door handle. • Keech's good friend owns CrauforD, an exclusive, small-production winery in Napa.

pored over his extensive collection of wine cellar design books. Nonetheless, "the space sort of naturally laid itself out," he says. At 10 feet wide by 16 feet long, the only issue was how to maximize capacity and minimize the "tunnel" look.

Keech and Warner decided on three arches that serve as display spaces. "The repetitious columns on the left and right made the room feel smaller, almost like a runway," Warner says. "The arches break it up and add interesting detail." The mirror backing also increases the feeling of expansiveness. "It adds depth to a cellar—really important in a long, narrow space like this," says Warner. "You get this sense of an infinity of wine bottles."

The arches did cost Keech space for more wine. "It's a thirteen-hundred-bottle cellar—I knew I wasn't going to go above that number. Keeping it down gave us wall space for the paintings and other art that we wanted." An added benefit is one removable arch: It hides a window through which furniture can be moved in and out.

The arches also display particularly prized bottles, like a 1955 Torres Gran Coronas. "That one was given to me by a friend who lost hundreds of bottles in the 1989 Loma Prieta earthquake," he says, obviously feeling his friend's pain. "You can be sure that one of my parameters for the cellar was not only that it be a great-looking space or have temperature control—it was going to be earthquake-proof to boot."

OPPOSITE, CLOCKWISE FROM TOP LEFT: Keech also stores an extensive cigar collection in his cellar. • "Walnut is a much harder wood [than redwood], and therefore trickier to work with," Warner says. • A prized bottle, a 1955 Torres Gran Coronas.

ABOVE, LEFT TO RIGHT: To highlight favorite bottles, Warner uses tiny LEDs on the double row of angled displays. • In addition to wine, Keech gets collecting tips from his good friend who owns CrauforD.

CELLAR SNAPSHOT

CAPACITY: 1,300
CRAUFORD
HOURGLASS
GEMSTONE
GHOST BLOCK
WILLIAMS SELYEM
PISONI
SEA SMOKE
1955 TORRES GRAN CORONAS

THE DAYS OF WINE AND BASEBALL

"THE OTHER NIGHT MY WIFE AND I WERE TALKING ABOUT HOW WE GOT INTO WINE," Rick Ryan, a software executive from the tony town of Weston, Massachusetts, says. "Sometimes I think it's because so many people in my industry are into it. Before we got married, in the late eighties, we'd drink a bottle of White Zinfandel every night. Now? If someone gave me a bottle of White Zin I'd throw it at 'em. But what can I say? Once we got used to drinking Bâtard-Montrachet, we couldn't go back."

After collecting commenced, storage space soon ran out. Ryan's first cellar was under the stairs. ("It wasn't temperature controlled or anything—my wife thought it was a little crazy.") Then he lined a small room with wine racks. That cellar grew to a tightly packed two thousand bottles. "So when we bought this house—it's our last house—at least I *hope* it's our last house—we decided to make room for the wine. At this point, there are four thousand bottles."

The cellar was to be part of an entertainment complex that includes a movie theater (complete with a concession area for popcorn and soda), a bar, and a billiard room. To kick off the design concept, he initially sat down with his architect, Thomas Catalano, and Fred Tregaskis of New England Wine Cellars. "I was after a very polished but lived-in look," Ryan says. Together they brainstormed and sketched ideas on the dining-room table, finally settling on a design. Ryan says, "I wanted a place where people could have a glass of wine but not have to be sitting in a fifty-five-degree room." So he set up a small, narrow tasting bar just outside the massive door. A small kitchen adjacent to the cellar not only holds glassware, decanters, and tableware, but also hides a dishwasher and two Sub-Zero under-counter refrigerators—"one for whites, another for Champagne"—under a rough-cut marble slab. At the head of this room is a painting he commissioned from artist Kerry Hellam, who shows his work at the Nantucket Wine Festival every year. "I'd met him at the festival and we got to talking; I don't remember whether this was an idea I had or if he suggested it," Ryan says. "He took labels I'd collected over a year from wines I'd consumed, and put them on the canvas, like a collage; then he painted a still life over it, but he made sure you could still see some of the labels."

OVERLEAF: The wine bottles envelop visitors to the cellar. Arches made of wine racks help organize Ryan's 4,000 bottles.

ABOVE LEFT TO RIGHT: A small, narrow tasting bar just outside the cellar allows guests to enjoy a glass of wine and not sit in a 55-degree room. • Rough-sawn beams from Liberty Cedar create a rustic look.

OPPOSITE: Oiled cherry wine racks are a burnished reddish hue and not one is left vacant. Long stretches of floor-to-ceiling space feature racking as well.

On the other side of the doors to the cellar is the main event: a clubby space, extremely masculine, with warm light thrown by three old, iron candle-style chandeliers, travertine stone, and massive posts and beams—8 by 8 slices of red cedar. Cedar is prized for its flexibility and its strength in proportion to its weight, as well as its natural resistance to humidity. "They took some time to find. We had to ship back the first ones that came in," Ryan recalls. "They were too polished; they didn't look natural enough." Liberty Cedar in Rhode Island finally offered the perfect solution— rough-sawn beams that give that just-so rustic look. Then Tregaskis slid oiled cherry wine racks that glow warmly with a burnished reddish hue into the mortises. No usable wall space is left unracked. Smallish rows rising halfway are put to work. Long stretches of floor-to-ceiling space are outfitted with racking as well. A library ladder allows complete access and receives constant use.

Ryan finds the case storage area a particular joy to have. Double-deep bins sit on rollers on the back wall of the

cellar; the whole wall can fit thirty wooden cases. Because those bins rise only halfway up the wall, plenty of counter space remains to show off special bottles. Then, rather than leave a solid, imposing wall of stone above the countertop, Tregaskis had an idea to carve out individual recesses—grottos—to fit large-format bottles, which Ryan loves. "They age a little better, and they're also really fun to take out when you're entertaining," he says, so three sections of wine racking have been devoted to these, which hold the bottles horizontally, label-out, for best viewing. The space is also where Ryan keeps wines with particularly meaningful personal associations. "They've all been signed by the wine-maker, or etched," he says. "They're special bottles, like an '88 Margaux—we were married in '88. Or a couple of

'91s; my first daughter was born in '91. There's a '95 Bollinger Grande Année for my second daughter. Another bottle is from a friend in London, a double magnum of Pol Roger bought at auction. It was signed by his granddaughter.

"My favorite wines have stories," he says. He finds that the personal connection makes them taste better. "Like this winery in Napa, Elan," he elaborates, referring to a boutique producer of highly allocated Cabs in Atlas Peak. "I had lunch with the owner, Patrick Elliott-Smith, a great guy who built his place from scratch. Now I'm on his mailing list."

Without a doubt, his favorite wine story is linked to another personal passion, baseball. "I'm an avid Red Sox fan," he says proudly. "Season's tickets, the whole deal. I was one of three fans selected by the Red Sox Foundation raffle

OPPOSITE: Above the case storage bins are individual recesses to fit large-format bottles and special collections. • Travertine stone highlights the red cedar and adds warmth and layered beauty to the cellar. • Ryan doesn't live on Bordeaux alone; California Cabernets are also part of his 4,000-bottle collection. • A small kitchen holds glassware, decanters, tableware, a dishwasher, and two Sub-Zero undercounter refrigerators.

ABOVE: In the back of the cellar is a case storage area that consists of double-deep bins placed on rollers. The whole wall can fit 30 wooden cases. • Rick Ryan with his Lafite Collection.

to win a 2004 Red Sox World Series ring. That year, 2004, was the first time the Red Sox had won since 1918. It was also the first time a professional sports team had allowed fans not associated with the team to receive rings. Obviously a big deal." Because of the 1918 association, he had already started his personal Bordeaux vertical homage to the Sox in Lafite. He then added a 2004. "Now, because the Red Sox won in 2007, when those are released I guess I'll have to get one of those as well," he says gleefully.

CELLAR SNAPSHOT

CAPACITY: 4,000 BOTTLES

1970 PETRUS

1982 BORDEAUX (LATOUR, CHEVAL BLANC, MARGAUX)

2000 BORDEAUX (FIRST GROWTHS AND SECOND GROWTHS)

CALIFORNIA CABERNETS (HARLAN ESTATE; ARAUJO ESTATE; MICHAEL GRACE; BRYANT; VERTICALS OF CAYMUS, CAYMUS SS, AND SILVER OAK; CHATEAU MONTELENA; OPUS ONE; INSIGNIA)

1918 LAFITE

2004 LAFITE

RIGHT: Red cedar is often used in wine cellars because it's flexible, strong, and resists humidity.

OPPOSITE: Ryan's passions are wine and baseball. "I'm an avid Red Sox fan," he says, and proudly displays his 1918 and 2004 Lafite in honor of their World Series victories.

A SOPHISTICATED PASSION

NEWPORT BEACH, CALIFORNIA

ON A 1968 CHRISTMAS LEAVE FROM HIS TOUR OF DUTY IN VIETNAM, Geoffrey (or Jeff, as he prefers to be called) Stack's sister presented him with a Time/Life book on wine and spirits. "Prior to that," he reminisces, "my idea of a great wine was Mateus and Lancers."

Perhaps it was an escape from the reality of war, but he found the concept of wine as a living, breathing, complex being, absolutely compelling. The next year, when Stack was out of the jungle and in Wharton business school, he discovered the school's wine club. He hadn't as yet made his financial mark in the world. There was relatively little he could do about seriously collecting. And so he pursued a more pocket-friendly pastime, reading and researching and buying middling Bordeaux. Somewhere along the line, the wine spark turned into a fire. As it turned out, it was also a literate connection to wine.

"When I had moved back to California," Stack says, "I saw an article about a wine store, Duke of Bourbon in Canoga Park, owned by David Breitstein. I went out to see him. He spent three hours with me on a Saturday morning and we were talking mostly about California wines. I didn't buy anything then, but the following week I bought my first full case of wine."

That first case turned out to be the N.V. Spring Mountain Vineyard Cabernet Sauvignon Lot H 68.69.LN, a blend of the 1968 and 1969 vintages, including grapes purchased from wine-maker Joe Heitz—a dinosaur with 12.5 percent alcohol on the label. It was the first Spring Mountain ever made. "It was labeled LH68-69 and it was five-fifty a bottle, minus the case discount. Even now, it only goes for about a hundred dollars a bottle, if you can find it, but it is still a beauty." Now there are only two bottles left of the case he had been nursing along. "One of them I'm saving for Breitsein to drink with me. I'll never open the other. I've bought lots of wine from him over the past thirty-six years. He really got me going."

There was one more crowning event, his introduction to older wine. His old partner bought a wine cellar, offered for a song in a real-estate deal. "He told me to take half of the cellar. There was some great old stuff that I still have. That propelled me more. It just sort of got out of hand."

An Old World feeling radiates from the cellar's brick-vaulted, Texas limestone–accented ceilings.

Out of hand? Without a question, that describes his current collection of sixteen thousand bottles. Though he's constantly buying and confesses to one-click buying that is all too easy on the Internet, he is mostly enjoying his older wines and buying them already aged-up when he can, such as from the Antique Wine Company in London. "I find that today, wines just aren't built to age, so I don't buy as many California."

For such an avid collector, Stack was late coming to his dream cellar. His previous one was placed in a reinvented coat closet and for quite a while most of his wines stayed in storage. In 2001, he and his wife bulldozed their old house to build a three-story French-Mediterranean style facing the rolling waves of Newport Beach, California. This time they wanted a different kind of wine storage, something that suggested the cellar in an older château. In their current cellar, that suggestion reads loudly from the first glimpse of the leaded stained-glass door that leads into the wine room. Once opened, the effect is a surprise that doesn't quit. Much like in the C. S. Lewis book *The Lion, the Witch, and the Wardrobe*, behind the door, it's an entirely different universe: 19 feet by 48 feet, and wine is everywhere.

The element that drives home the Old World feeling is the brick-vaulted, Texas limestone–accented ceilings, ever so

PAGE 116: A round table bisects this room—one side for red wine, one side for white.

ABOVE: Benoit installed special shelves to showcase Stack's favorites in secret corners of the cellar. • "I am still having so much fun even though I know I have far more wine than I can ever drink. But that,

too, is terrific because that offers plenty of opportunity to donate some terrific wine," says Stack.

OPPOSITE: A leaded stained-glass door that opens to the wine room embodies Old World charm.

suggestive of Guastavino's grand efforts for New York City's Oyster Bar. This cellar cleverly sidesteps the pitfall of a visual blur of wood racking. There is a flow to the room, thanks to a dance of rectangles, diamonds, and squares, all subtly placed to avoid any sense of busyness. Acting as an anchor are floor-to-ceiling wine cascades, so grand they are more like escalators weighed down with large-format bottles.

The room is separated into two lobes—one for red wine, one for white—bisected with a round table, which usually serves as the focal point during cocktail hour or post-dinner party. All about are diamond bins. "I wanted those bins. But frankly, Ben Benoit, my designer, wasn't wild about them. Though I like the way they look, that wasn't all. The shape enables me to have six bottles of one kind of wine in one place, making it easy to pull."

The cellar is relatively low-tech, which means temperature control at a lower degree than usual, 52 degrees, in order to slow down the older wines' aging process. Currently, Stack uses no software to track the wines. "I really don't need it," he explains. "I know where everything is because I placed every bottle myself." And in keeping with his Old World approach,

CELLAR SNAPSHOT

CAPACITY: 16,000 BOTTLES
NAPA VALLEY SPRING MOUNTAIN
CABERNET SAUVIGNON LOT H 68.69.LN
1943 CHÂTEAU CARBONNIEUX "GRAVES BORDEAUX"
1959 CHÂTEAU LATOUR HAUT-BRION
LAFITE ROTHSCHILD
OREGON PINOT NOIRS

he has an actual log, kept on that round table. "The same way I placed every bottle, I log in, on a daily basis, what goes in and out. My secretary plugs it into an Excel program. But I might cave in to modern times. We're looking at a larger computer program right now."

After all these bottles and years, does he get bored? "I am still having so much fun, even though I know I have far more wine than I can ever drink. But that, too, is terrific because it offers me plenty of opportunity to donate some terrific wine." Similar to many collectors, he puts together the random case or two for charity auctions, but the Stacks also have their own foundation for the Cystinosis Research Foundation. "When I go," he says, "the proceeds of the cellar will fund the foundation. There is more wine here than I can drink in a lifetime and it makes me feel very gratified that after I pass, it will support a very good cause."

OPPOSITE: Wine cascades visually bisect the room and cleverly accommodate large-format bottles.

ABOVE LEFT TO RIGHT: Sixteen thousand bottles crammed into a 19' x 48' space guarantee that wine is everywhere. • Stack collaborated carefully with designer Ben Benoit to achieve his dream cellar.

RENAISSANCE MAN

HOLLYWOOD HILLS, CALIFORNIA

FOR TELEVISION AND RADIO HOST RYAN SEACREST, HOME IS A SPACIOUS MEDITERRANEAN-STYLE VILLA in the Hollywood Hills known as Casa di Pace, or House of Peace. While previous owners Kevin Costner and Richard Dreyfuss did not install a wine cellar, carving out a space for one became Seacrest's top priority. He handed over the job to Jeff Andrews, a choreographer-turned-designer, with these instructions: "I wanted the wine-cellar design to be on par with the rest of my home, a mix of European influences coupled with a certain sense of Old Hollywood glamour. I wanted it functional, to the point, yet personal and meaningful." He was extremely eager to move his wine from off-site storage and under his own roof.

While other fathers and sons bond over golf, Seacrest and his father bonded over the mysteries and pleasures of wine. Now, most people know him as the host of *American Idol*; others know him as a frequent figure on the California auction route. He is quick to rattle off the wines he's enjoying: Rosé Champagne, especially Krug, and Dom Pérignon, Big Napa Cabernets, and well chosen Bordeaux, not all of which are

first and second growths; he gets enjoyment out of wines like Château Palmer as well. Top Burgundies such as Domaine Leroy are also strong magnets. But in the summer, it's Rosé that he enjoys most of the time, especially Domaines Ott Rosé and Whispering Angel.

Seeking the right space for the project, Andrews zeroed in on the downstairs recreation room, where in addition to the bar and tasting area, he created a separate room-within-a room for the cellar. This was the size of a small New York City studio apartment. "The trick," he says, "was to make it seem as if the cellar had been there, as if it had a history, and to bring in a taste of the Old World. But the house, built in the '70s, was not exactly Old World. Making the cellar look permanent, and not like a stage set, was a challenge until Andrews found what he was looking for: four-hundred-year-old French terra-cotta tiles. "The day I found them, I knew they would make all the difference. I themed the whole room around the terra-cotta, virtually turning it into a brick-toned box."

He fit the tiles together in a herringbone pattern, slathering them like icing on the floors and ceiling. In a flight of creativity, he chose to put in a paneled ceiling

made of Honduras mahogany, also used on the arched, Spanish, medieval-like door. Why stop with those reds? He decided to layer more in, including the brick-red paint and straightforward, utilitarian redwood racking.

The design team worked closely together; cellar designer Jean France Mercier was the utilitarian voice that shaped Andrews's aesthetic. "This was my first wine-cellar design," Andrews explains, "and there was a learning curve. Jean France guided me through the standard do's and don'ts. I needed to adjust to the facts, like exactly how much room was I going to lose because of the cooling system? Were there certain stains and finishes I couldn't use because they put the bottles at risk?"

The hardest design dream to give up was natural light. "Mercier nixed the idea, teaching me how it endangered the wines." Andrews recounted that he compromised and opted for a window on the hallway side, floor-to-ceiling and arched similarly to the mahogany door.

In turn, Andrews influenced the wine-racking shape and choices. Seacrest wanted a straightforward system but there was room to play with the ground-level racking. "The line really needed to be broken up with so much gridwork around."

Andrews's stylistic touches add great charm to the room. Antique barrel-back chairs, for some in-cellar tastes, and the delicate table make the space homey. He produced a copy

OVERLEAF: Seacrest wanted his cellar to be "a mix of European influences coupled with a certain sense of Old Hollywood glamour."

ABOVE: Andrews added antique barrel-back chairs, luscious upholstered leather seating, and the delicate table. • Andrews themed the room around 400-year-old French terra-cotta tiles.

ABOVE: In Seacrest's recreation room, Andrews designed a bar and tasting area and created a separate room-within-a-room for the cellar. • The tiles were fit together in a herringbone pattern on the floors and ceiling.

of an antique Spanish iron lantern that broadcasts a very soft, pure light over the tasting area. One of Seacrest's favorite aspects is the built-in breakfront in the cellar's "L." This particular piece is completely inventive, as the interior is customized for perfect, safe stemware storage. Each glass bin is cut to accommodate each particular shape, from flute to balloon.

Living through construction, waiting for the project to come together, often seemed interminable but now that Seacrest and his friends have enjoyed many glasses together, he can look back and talk about it all as an adventure. "Everything about it was terrific. The design, the feel, the process—but most of all, that all those bottles in that room are mine to share. Wine is emotional and meaningful to me. When we started out, I was after a design that could communicate its importance. We got there."

CELLAR SNAPSHOT

CAPACITY: 3,500
ROSÉ CHAMPAGNE, KRUG, AND DOM PÉRIGNON
BIG NAPA CABERNETS
CHÂTEAU PALMER
DOMAINE LEROY
DOMAINES OTT ROSÉ
WHISPERING ANGEL

PART III

THE SYBARITE'S SANCTUARY

Sybarites are all about luxury, and in these spaces exalted Burgundies are not the only coveted objects on display. Magnificent materials, including rugged wood timbers, exotic marbles, and mahogany compete for the limelight. The use of such rich materials in spaces that were long adorned with nothing fancier than plywood, stone, and concrete is a solid indicator that wine is no longer relegated to the dingy basement or to basement-quality materials. Here, the wine cellar is a showpiece in its own right.

Often design elements that are typically only found in more public, high-traffic areas appear in these cellars. Beveled iron doors with jewel-like cuts of glass, venetian plaster in butter or red metallic hues, even a custom Swarovski crystal chandelier such as the one found in New York City's Cooper-Hewitt Museum, highlight these spaces and expand the traditional boundaries of cellar design. Down to their very bones, these cellars are lavish: Sleek, dark wood and custom furniture exemplify the exotic, the beautiful, and the affluent.

And for many, the ultimate object of desire in today's environmentally conscious times is to create a gorgeous green cellar.

ODE TO SAKE

BRIDGEHAMPTON, NEW YORK

"WHEN SOME MEN SAY "MY WIFE GOT THE HOUSE," IT IMPLIES A CERTAIN BLEAK SCENARIO. But when happily married oenophile Michael Brown says it, he is actually referring to a clever division of labor. He and his wife came to an agreement while building their Bridgehampton mansion: She had free rein over the general design while he got to call the shots in the wine cellar. A new convert to the ways of wine, he carefully plotted out every little detail with delight, aided by cellar designer Lee Zinser.

For the living spaces, his wife drew inspiration from the breezy, refreshingly ivory-and-white palette of Diane Keaton's character's home in the film *Something's Gotta Give*. Downstairs, his own references were drawn from a number of sources but in the end he ended up commingling the aesthetics of a men's haberdasher with the American Museum of Natural History. The result is monolithic and striking. Brown wanted a dramatic, historic atmosphere, but as he says, "The good news is that everything inside is drinkable."

Some of the parameters Brown handed over to Zinser arose from the homeowner's fanaticism for Japanese food and its most delicious sidekick, sake.

Sake bottles are not only oddly shaped, but they also require a lower-than-typical wine-cellar temperature for storage. Because the Browns have a constant stream of weekend guests, their entertaining needs are significant. At the top of the list is an abundance of chilled wines and sakes on demand. That all translated into the need for refrigeration.

Wine refrigerators, however, are not among Zinser's list of favorite cellar items. "The whole reason to have a wine cellar," the designer explains, "is to avoid refrigerators. But in a case like this where they couldn't be avoided, the issue was more how to turn the situation into a thing of beauty."

Zinser presented Brown with sketches. He liked them. The construction commenced.

The expanse of floor-to-ceiling glass doors opens with a touch of the owner's finger, and when they part, visitors have the sense of stepping inside a diorama entitled "A Gentleman's Wine Cellar." Dark mahogany covers the 25-by-15-foot room, adding gravitas. Lighting is something Zinser takes seriously; at night, especially, the room glows sexily, enhanced by the way the lighting plays on the orange hues and teases the

sensual amber-colored door pulls. Using pinpointed lighting to direct the eye, he created a special place for those refrigerators, also setting them off by framing them with a slight arch in the ceiling. Rich African mahogany lines the passage. On the left of the vestibule, shelves hold stemware and a decanting table. On the right are the wines cooled to perfection in the refrigerators. By angling certain bottles, Zinser gave the wines and sakes more of a presentational look, so they blend more organically into the display of the cellar.

Past the refrigerator-cum-light display, a large case dominates the heart of the room. Easily mistaken for an

extravagant lepidopterist's case, a quick look through the glass reveals the real content: Instead of pinned butterflies, some of Brown's most prized bottles are on view. His selection is constantly changing; That's part of his fun. Currently he is enjoying showing off pedigree bottles in magnums, and their smaller, standard-sized, 750-milliliter mates, such as the 2004 Harlan Estates, or Sine Qua Non, two of his current favorites.

A savvy businessman who recently sold his previous operation to OfficeMax, Brown now owns a sustainable-storage-solution company. While he isn't much of a collector in other aspects, he has taken to wine like a duck to water.

OVERLEAF: Brown displays his most prized bottles as if they were precious artifacts pinned and butterflied in an extravagant lepidopterist's case.

ABOVE: Brown needed a cellar that would accommodate his love for sake. • Ivory and white in the living spaces contrast with the cellar's dark, moody interiors.

OPPOSITE: To build his 3,000-bottle collection Brown buys two cases at a time: one for himself to drink now, one to either resell or age up.

The 25' x 15' room is made of dark mahogany illuminated with custom lighting.

The refrigerators that store the sake are set apart like sculpture through pinpointed lighting and framed by a slight arch in the ceiling.

He thanks his brother-in-law for sharing the bug. In fact, he says all of the men in his family have been bitten by it. "Between my father, brothers, and brother-in-law, we probably buy between eight and ten really special bottles a year."

Acting with tremendous speed, Brown built his three-thousand-bottle collection in less than a year. His strategy? Buying two cases at a time: one for himself to drink now, one to either resell or age up. The bulk of his wines are from California. "Along with sake, I'm a California Cab guy. But lately, I've fallen in love with Grenache."

A self-described gadget-lover, he employed plenty of bells and whistles in the cellar. "The greatest thing that is going," he says, "is that while I haven't bar-coded my bottles,

everything that has to do with that room is controlled by software."

For example, to make sure no one can get their hands on some of the more precious bottles, such as when his children are old enough to cause some real mischief, he's installed fingerprinting control for room access. "No one gets in there unless they come to me first." For ease, electronic tablets containing his wine inventory are strategically placed all over the house. Right now he is using the VinCellar software from VinFolio. This particular program shows the location, quantity, and even the label images of the wines in his cellar. "My guests," says the mid-thirties Brown, "can scroll through all of my bottles. They can also check out the reviews, posted

ABOVE LEFT TO RIGHT: "I wanted a gorgeous display. This is my room," says Brown. • Floor-to-ceiling glass doors open using fingerprint technology. • Zinser angles certain bottles so they blend more organically into the display of the cellar.

OPPOSITE: Brown enjoys constantly changing his display case. Beneath the display area is plenty of storage for cases of his latest acquisition.

by the VinFolio members online, and then decide what bottle they would like me to open next."

Brown isn't sure how far he will take his collection. Sure, the whites and sakes need constant stocking, but he thinks that the three-thousand-bottle point is probably sufficient. "I had plenty of room to play with in the house," he said. "I could have placed twenty thousand bottles in there. But more than volume, I wanted a gorgeous display. This is my room," he says, emphasizing the "my." "I really wanted my guests to admire it, and to see everything from the outside. It is my private domain, even if it is an open book." Then he adds with a shake of his head, "You know, it took as long to build this room as the rest of the house."

CELLAR SNAPSHOT

CAPACITY: 3,000 BOTTLES

PEDIGREE BOTTLES IN MAGNUMS AND THEIR SMALLER, STANDARD-SIZE, 750-MILLILITER MATES, SUCH AS THE 2004 HARLAN ESTATE, OR SINE QUA NON

SAKE

GRENACHE

GOING GREEN

INVERNESS, CALIFORNIA

WHEN LYNN FRAME AND HER HUSBAND, RICK HOSKINS, BOUGHT A WEEKEND PLACE near the spectacular Point Reyes coast, they were adamant about finding an environmentally friendly way to build a better wine cellar. Their ideal system would passively preserve their wines at a safe temperature, meaning they would never have to click any switches or pull any levers that increased their carbon footprint. The couple was fiercely determined to keep their wine collection at the ready for any entertaining situation, yet still keep the bottles safe from harm.

Hoskins, a principal with a private-equity firm, says that they started collecting in the early '90s when Frame brought him two EuroCave wine coolers. "We loved wine, but at that point our way of going about it changed and we started to prepare for the joys of aging wine." Eventually they inched up to two thousand bottles, mostly reds. While they adore Bordeaux, they also look for wines from diverse regions of France, Italy, and Argentina. Raised in Germany, Hoskins has devoted a good part of the collection to Riesling. "In all fairness, the cellar project was driven by Lynn," he says. An officer in Slow Food USA, an organization that promotes authenticity—meaning food that is chemical- and additive-free, made with few shortcuts and plenty of Old-World charm—Frame is fierce about being environmentally cautious. "She was insistent that we just couldn't buy a house, renovate according to our principles—going as far as to plant greenery on the house's roof for insulation—and then blow our cover on an energy-hog of a wine cellar. We just couldn't have lived with the hypocrisy if that was the place. We'd have thrown our hands up."

Wine is a considerable financial and emotional investment, and heat and humidity can wreak havoc with bottle quality. While these elements were of concern, the couple nixed the idea of building out the house to make a new room for a special wine cellar because they only use it every other weekend. Instead, they set out to find a piece of the 1950s dwelling to co-opt. "In our search we realized we had only one option. Though it was ugly, it could work," Hoskins remembers thinking. They found themselves staring at a bunker-type room built into the house's foundation and accessed through a staircase off the family room. "It had been a cement storage room of some sort, quite

small, only five by fifteen, and exceedingly dirty, with plenty of exposed nail tips coming out of the ceiling. So being tall as I am, six foot one, I had to be careful not to scrape my scalp." They consulted their friend Alan Abrams, of Alan Abrams Wine Designs, and realized the room could be the answer to their dilemma. But first they had to take the room's temperature.

For eight months they monitored it and were thrilled with the verdict. The fluctuation was moderate, a mere three degrees. The lowest temperature was fifty-seven degrees Fahrenheit and the warmest, sixty. "Sure, it was a less-than-ideal situation. Plenty of purists would turn their noses up at

us, saying a cellar should be a perfect fifty-five degrees. But we knew the collection wouldn't be ruined. Perhaps the wines would mature at a faster pace, but that's not such a bad thing. We could live with the solution."

The owners were prepared for a bare-bones functional room, ready to accept lack of beauty in place of virtue, but when Abrams presented his sketch, they saw that they didn't have to compromise. Elevated by vintage-y woodwork and a combination of curves and angles, it was anything but dull. The wine shelves are built around an arch, with a solid, Stickley-esque feel. The warmth from the choice of wood, redwood, was to be a key element, but the sourcing of the

OVERLEAF: "We wanted someone who would not judge us for having a passive cellar. Someone who would work with no air-conditioning and someone who could find certified, reclaimed redwood to build the racking and shelving. You'd think we were looking for an illegal substance, it was so difficult," opines Hoskins.

ABOVE: The owners liked the idea that the imperfection of the cellar's materials would contrast with the smooth bottles. • Reclaimed redwood was used for warmth. • "In our search we realized we had only one option. Though it was ugly, it could work," the owner says of building a bunker into the house's foundation.

wood was another problem, as the owners mandated that no new trees should be cut down for their shelves. "You'd think in a region with such green awareness as the Bay Area it would be simple. It was not," Frame says.

Finding the right builder was the next obstacle. "We wanted someone who would not judge us for having a passive cellar. Someone who would work with no air-conditioning, and someone who could find certified, reclaimed redwood to build the racking and shelving. You'd think we were looking for an illegal substance, it was so difficult." Abrams put them in touch with Tom Warner. The Walnut Creek–based wine-cellar builder knew how to obtain the wood and was also philosophically connected to green design as well as to wine. In fact, Warner uses reclaimed materials whenever possible. Warner understood Frame's and Hoskins's committment to green design. And the stars were in alignment for success.

The beauty of a passive cellar lies in how little effort it requires to work properly. The solar power ensures plenty of replenishable energy for light. Controlling mold is easy, especially with a lot of concrete, but just in case, Warner installed an air-purifying system that zaps airborne mold spores and removes odors from the cellar. In keeping with their vision, the system activates with a flick of the energy-efficient lightbulb every time Rick goes in to pick out some bottles.

Hoskins was in great need of a few more inches for head clearance, a need that initiated the complicated task of digging a new floor. Concrete was repoured, and as Tom Warner explains of the result, "It was a blessing to have at

ABOVE LEFT TO RIGHT: The wine shelves echo Mission furniture and are built around an arch. • The woodwork and a combination of curves and angles add style to the space.

least one level surface in the room, because hiding the many wall protrusions and incorporating the wall's bumps and curves into the design was a little sticky."

Some raw edges remained naturally in the concrete and some electrical cables stayed exposed. Frame and Hoskins were happy to accept these imperfections, believing them to provide an interesting aesthetic counterpoint to the smooth, round surfaces of the bottles. In fact, they are more than happy with their storage solution. "We really like that raw, natural look," says Frame, "but truly, the woodwork acts as furniture, and the beauty of the wood and bottles dominates the room. We find the whole project amazing. At first it looked tiny, cramped, and dark, and now it's a treasure box."

CELLAR SNAPSHOT

CAPACITY: 650
1998 PETRUS
2004 GUNDERLOCH
RIESLING TROCKEN

ABOVE: "Truly, the woodwork acts as furniture and the beauty of the wood and bottles dominates the room. We find the whole project amazing. It first looked tiny, cramped, and dark and now it's a treasure box," says Hoskins.

OPPOSITE: The owner saw that they didn't have to compromise to have a green cellar. This cellar passively preserves wines at a safe temperature without increasing the home's carbon footprint. • "We really like that raw, natural look, " says Lynn Hoskins of the raw edges that remained naturally in the concrete.

THE MAN CAVE

SIMI VALLEY, CALIFORNIA

ANDY HEYNEMAN, A SOUTHERN CALIFORNIA RETAIL EXECUTIVE, BLUNTLY DESCRIBES THE SANCTUARY that houses his favorite material objects with two words: "man cave." "In fact, my wife jokes that proper chromosomes are needed in order to pass over the threshold," he says.

Just in case any questions remain about the kind of bonding that goes on within its walls, customized M&M's emblazoned with the words "man cave" are there to resolve them. And in this space, mere meters from their home, on five acres in the Ventura section of Los Angeles, Heyneman has created an extravagant entertainment complex. There are rooms for music—listening and playing, complete with a drum set; a sitting area; a full kitchen; a billiards room; a bar; and a wine cellar. Next to the cellar is a garage that displays a dazzling collection of fourteen vintage cars.

Though Heyneman was born in Cairo, he has lived in California his entire life. He readily admits his love lies with California wines, mostly those from Napa. "It starts out like this," Andy recounts. "You get a bottle of Cabernet on the way to the grocery store. Then there are four bottles at any given time near the dish rack.

Then you graduate to a wine closet. At that point all hell breaks loose; your buying is out of control. Then you hire someone to build a proper cellar."

This is the second cellar that the Los Angeles cellar designer Ben Benoit has built for him. "The first one was underground and I had to access it from the outside," Heyneman says. "It was weird. The home's previous owner had installed an imposing bank safe–like door in the room. Regardless of the karma, I had some great times in that space Ben reinvented for me." However, he did notice that his wines tasted somewhat musty from the storage belowground. That was one reason Heyneman felt his new cellar needed to be at street level.

When Heyneman and his wife saw the new potential home, they knew they had lucked out. His wife got the view and acreage she wanted; he got his hideaway. "I was very psyched. When I saw the space, I immediately started to tear down the walls with my inner eye," he remembers. Passing from the billiards room, with its sharp modernity, into the darkened cave of the wine bar/cellar area makes it clear that Heyneman has achieved his goal of cave-aesthetic-meets-1930s–Palm Springs elegance.

OVERLEAF: Both an aesthetic and a sentimental choice, the stone counter is the same kind of marble used in their old home, but in a different color.

ABOVE: The passageway from the billiards room into the wine area is framed by scorched, distressed oak timber. • Made of rough bleached sandstone, the interior wall is illuminated by votives perched on small stones.

OPPOSITE: Rich materials and accents abound in the dark mahogany floors, clubby stools, and bar made of green marble from the Brazilian rain forest.

Distressed oak timber, scorched to a darkened look by propane, frames the passageway from the billiard room into the wine area. As if walking through the mouth of a cave, the temperature drops, the smell changes, the light plays against the rough bleached sandstone interior wall. Mood-changing, flickering votives are perched on stones stepped-out from the wall. The effect is haunting and audible, as if a piano were plinking in the background. Wide-plank, dark mahogany floorboards support the clubby stools at the stunning bar made of green marble from the Brazilian rain forest. Heyneman chose the stone in part for its beauty and in part because of its complex terrazzo-like appearance which, with bits of stone trapped in its facade, almost seems reminiscent of bottle corks.

The couple had used the same kind of marble in a different color in their old home. In the man cave, hand-blown Murano-glass light fixtures in fluid shapes, echoing a Dali-esque clock, drip over the bar. At the bar, up to fifteen manly men can gather, happy wine explorers who gaze

with thirst at the glass-enclosed wine cellar before them. "I love telling friends to go into the cellar and bring out something they like. The only time I would tell them no," he says generously, "is if the wine isn't ready."

For convenience when entertaining, they've installed a sink, garbage disposal, and one of Heyneman's favorite additions, a Riedel glass–safe dishwasher that cools off the wineglasses so no one ever gets a hot one. An impromptu wine-and-cheese event at eleven thirty at night is not uncommon. Neither is a friend who tries to walk through the crystal-clear glass of the door to the cellar. "I think my friends are so dazzled by the sight of all those bottles that they forget about the door," Heyneman says, laughing. When there are a lot of bottles being uncorked or more than a handful of people, he tacks a note on the door saying, "Be careful of your nose!"

Once Heyneman's bar-area concept was executed, he gave Benoit free rein on the design. After all, the two had known each other for ten years and had shared many a bottle. Benoit knew what his friend wanted, such as being able to gaze lovingly at all of those bottles from the bar. "Then we moved a wall or two and ended up with a space that was twenty-two feet long and eight feet deep. I wanted rustic and functional for him. Keep it to the point, all about the wine and stacking ease. In that cellar, on those

LEFT: The cellar is part of an entertainment complex, complete with a room for music, a sitting area, a full kitchen, a billiards room, and a bar.

alder-wood racks, are every heavy California producer in the state," Benoit says.

The designer built in cascade racking to frame the window of the cellar. The image created has pyramidal importance and is a great solution for showing off those heavy-hitters and bigger bottles. At nighttime, the racks get backlit for extra drama. A lot of racking can become dizzying, so Benoit broke up the space with a running stripe of that distinctive emerald-y marble. More than just a flash of color, the slabs serve as functional countertops.

Heyneman's three-thousand-bottle inventory is computerized, but as far as order? "Let's just say I have a loose sense of where things go," he says. He segregates the bottles by region, vintage, and varietal. But most important, he keeps his reds on the right and his whites, mostly French, on the left.

A fateful visit to France shaped his taste for them. "Once I got lost while on vacation, which is my favorite way to make discoveries. A wine shop owner invited me to breakfast. The next day I was drinking espresso with him at seven a.m. in this tiny square in Burgundy, and he was introducing me to some smaller appellations that are rare in the United States."

His wife, while absolutely wine-friendly, keeps her drinking restricted to the house except on special nights when the women are invited over to the sacred cave sanctum. "My wife is predominantly focused on Pinots," Heyneman

ABOVE: Large-format bottles take center stage on cascade racking that frames the window of the cellar. • Heyneman aspired to have a swanky billiards room that harkened to Palm Springs style of the 1930s.

OPPOSITE: The racks are made from alder wood and they contain offerings from "every heavy California producer in the state," designer Benoit says.

says. He shares that to make life easy for her, he put together her own personal wine rack for the house. "But," he adds, "if I've been negligent and not kept it full, she knows how to get my attention. She basically takes one of my really good bottles each day and holds those soldiers hostage. She'll grab something, unaware of what it represents. I deny my wife nothing, nothing at all. But she sticks a knife through my heart when she pinches a 1991 Quintessa or a similar vintage Bryant, pours a glass, and leaves it three-fourths full. Ouch. It's turned into an unspoken signal for when it's time for me to refill the rack. You know? It works really well!"

CELLAR SNAPSHOT

CAPACITY: 3,885 BOTTLES

LEONETTI

KEN WIGHT PINOT

ALBAN GRENACHE

WHITE COTTAGE BOUTIQUE WINE BY DENNIS AND ADELE JOHNS

MAGNUM OF 2004 LEWIS CELLARS RESERVE CABERNET

THE CATHEDRAL OF WINE

SONOMA, CALIFORNIA

"JOHN AND I CALL IT THE CATHEDRAL OF WINE," SAYS NANCY LASSETER with a smile, referring to her cellar and her husband, the creator of the wildly inventive, joy-giving Pixar animations.

Because of the fanciful aspect to John's design work, one would expect this particular couple to have wine storage laced with plenty of clever touches, and it does not disappoint. The whole house, designed by Backen Gillam Architects, is a showpiece. From the water park outside, which delights their five boys, to the wine cellar that charms the couple themselves, the wow factor is huge.

"When we moved to Sonoma in 1991, we had an interest in wine but not in the wine business," Lasseter says. Some years later, her housekeeper came in one day with purple-stained hands. She had been picking grapes. "I thought that sounded like a lot of fun and went along the next time. I came home covered in Zinfandel juice and was hooked." In 2005 they acquired a winery in Glen Ellen, not far from this home, and renamed it the Lasseter Family Vineyards.

By the time the Lasseters started work on their new home, they already had plenty of beloved wines that needed safekeeping. They had learned the hard way a few years earlier during a wine-cellar disaster. Their HVAC system crashed and about a thousand bottles fried in the heat. The Lasseters vowed that their next wine cellar would have a backup for such a worst-case scenario. So in addition to a geothermal heat-exchange system, a green solution that uses underground natural sources independent of electricity for keeping the room cool, they installed a conventional cooling system for those worst-case scenarios. According to Josh Rowland, the designer on the project, Lasseter came equipped with plenty of other thoughts on what she wanted for the cellar. "She was an extremely hands-on client with distinct ideas, from the use of ironwork to the way bottles should be racked, as well as ideas about the lighting."

As Nancy pulls open the heavily beveled glass-and-iron door, she explains that her inspiration for it came from her love of the ironwork found in the New Orleans Garden District. "See how the beveled glass shines? It's as if it was made up of jewels." The UV-treated glass shimmers like square-cut diamonds from the natural light that pours into the wine cellar. Beyond the jewel-like door, the wine cellar extends over a long sweep. Ceilings are twelve feet high. Plaster arches; saturated,

Designer Rowland decided to use plaster for the arches instead of brick because it "looked so beautiful, so clean, so perfect."

The space is warmed by the bricklike, tumbled limestone on the floor, the canary and koa wood lining the shelving units, and the Marmarino plaster in a Mediterranean sunny yellow.

PAGE 152: Tobias Wong created the dramatic chandelier with Swarovski crystal and a huge black lampshade. Owner Nancy Lasseter commissioned this piece after seeing Wong's work at the Cooper-Hewitt National Design Museum.

OPPOSITE, CLOCKWISE FROM TOP LEFT: The Lasseters' display includes many special and signed bottles—especially whimsical selections with graphics from Pixar films. • The 12-foot-high ceilings, plaster arches, saturated buttery-colored walls, and bays off the aisle evoke a Spanish monastery. • The heavily beveled glass-and-iron door was inspired by Lasseter's love of ironwork in the garden district of New Orleans.

buttery walls; and bays off the aisle suggest a glistening Spanish monastery, along with those doors and some spectacular lighting.

The room is shaped like a bolt. Three bays on either side of the stem hold wines that are grouped by varietal, held presentationally in steel racks fastened into exotic wood. At the head of the bolt hangs a planetary object that demands attention: a stunning crystal chandelier. "John and I saw a similar one at the Cooper-Hewitt Museum in New York City. We just had to commission one like it," Nancy says. Unquestionably dramatic, a tangle of Swarovski crystal peeks out of a huge black lampshade like a white frill under a black petticoat. Created by Tobias Wong as a riff on the Louisiana theme, the glittering piece is aptly called "New Orleans."

While Nancy's vision for the iron and the crystal were unwavering, any large project is likely to go through many permutations. This one was no different. For example, architect Chuck Covell recalls that the initial concept was to install brick arches. "We had some challenges finding the brick. Then we went with brick tile. Then we had some plaster. We did a test and decided the plaster looked so beautiful, so clean, so perfect, that we went with that for the arches. The floor tile was supposed to be something else as well. Initially we were using some tile from Belgium. But when we started to lay it down there was an awful smell we couldn't identify and we were really puzzled. One day it was stacked out on the site, in the heat. That's when we saw that the tiles were actually oozing. We found out they had been stored inside of a factory, soaking up oil, for years and years. There went that idea. But as a result we decided on something even better, especially since we were going with the clean plaster: limestone that has been tumbled to give it an antique finish." The limestone floors were designed to create a different pattern in the aisles than in the sanctuary.

Air-cooling ventilation in this high-concept, elegant room is anything but pedestrian. To disguise the HVAC details, there are ten pieces of ironwork—laser-cut grates with patterns that include swirls and medallions, vaguely recalling the master Edgar Brandt's Deco ironwork pieces. Form plays well off function. In other areas, the aesthetic choice has triumphed over efficiency, such as in the Lasseters' decision to display

bottles horizontally to show their labels clearly. The family has many special and signed bottles, and along with the regular Lasseter Family label, they also design labels with colorful Pixar graphics—which add a lot of fun to an otherwise formal and spare room. Even with their choice of display, there is still room for six thousand bottles and two hundred magnums. "We didn't count bottles when we started. That was a mistake," Nancy says. "We underestimated how many large-format bottles we actually had. When the racking was used up, we had to dismantle several of the bottom rungs to make room. Obviously we felt a little silly."

Fortunately it was all fixable, and the room does not suffer from the adjustment. With steel, iron, and crystal as the backbone of the room, the Lasseters and Rowland were careful to incorporate warmer elements for balance. The brick-like, tumbled limestone on the floor, the canary and koa wood

ABOVE, LEFT TO RIGHT: Laser-cut grates with swirls and medallions disguise the HVAC details. The patterns are inspired by master Edgar Brandt's Deco ironwork pieces. • To the right of the chandelier stands a wall of wines that is a secret passage to Lasseter's project room, where she does the boxing and shipping for their own label of wines. • Lasseter Family Vineyards was founded in 2005.

OPPOSITE: Access to the cellar from the inside of the house is reached via a wall that looks like a normal bookcase. On that bookcase is a ledge. And on that ledge is a book. And in that book is the fingerprint control to enter.

lining the shelving units, and the Marmarino plaster in a Mediterranean sunny yellow make the room look like an inviting still life.

Reflecting on the project, Josh Rowland says that as they got deeper into the process, a design concept revealed itself. "The room also became about secret places. So much is hidden. The Geo Therm, the venting behind the grates, the chandelier hidden under its shade, and even some of the wines are almost hidden from sight, nestled in their bays."

But for a visitor, the most interesting design element is the cellar's biggest secret. To the right of the chandelier stands a wall of wines. Nancy walks over to it and stares at the stacked bottles, trying to remember. "Oh, it's this one," she says, turning a bottle as if were a doorknob. The wall moves, and in a few seconds she and her visitor are standing on the other side of it, no longer in the wine cellar but in her project room, where she also does the boxing and shipping for the family's own label. From the other side, inside the house, the wall looks like a normal bookcase. On that bookcase is a ledge, and on that ledge is a book, and in that book is the fingerprint control used to gain access to the wine cellar. "We had to find Creative Home Engineering, an Arizona company specializing in secret doors. Isn't it amazing?"

Her visitor responds in the affirmative.

"I'm so sorry," she said. "I'm rambling on like a proud parent. But isn't it just the best space?"

CELLAR SNAPSHOT

CAPACITY: 6,000 BOTTLES AND 200 MAGNUMS
1994 GRACE FAMILY CABERNET SAUVIGNON

THE LUXE LIFE

WHILE THE MASTER OF INTERIOR DESIGN, BILLY BALDWIN, MAY HAVE SUGGESTED STARTING ROOM DESIGN FROM THE RUG UP, in the case of this Connecticut Maine-style shingle house, designer Michael Whaley started from the ceiling down. The reversal started when his forty-something clients, who were in the process of building their waterfront house, asked him to examine its lower level and help them to decide how to organize the complex of game and socializing rooms they had in mind. When Whaley explored the raw space, he was struck by a section of the expanse with an extraordinarily high ceiling. Staring up, he envisioned dramatic, double-vaulted ceilings. His next vision? Wine bottles. That was it. He wanted to build an extraordinary wine cellar. Whaley got his way even though the couple were not serious wine drinkers. However, many of their friends liked wine, and some of them loved fine wine. The owners saw it not only as a way to cater to their friends when entertaining but also as an opportunity to learn more about wine while they started their own collection. They signed on for the idea with tremendous gusto.

Whaley then approached the house's architect, Scott Raissis, to fashion the arches, ones that were worthy of Renaissance Europe. Once installed, they created a magnificent frame for the wine cellar and set the mood. The resulting visual could easily be a hideaway for royalty. In fact, Bonnie Prince Charlie would not have felt out of place in such a setting.

Looking to the Old World for design seemed natural. The clients had lived in England, frequented France, and loved the French wines that, in anticipation of their new wine lifestyle, they had begun sourcing from the Westchester wine store Zachy's. To invoke a sense of ambience, Whaley created furniture riffing on a bygone era, such as the room's centerpiece, an eighteenth-century-style French-walnut tasting table. Its tabletop design features inlaid planks of contrasting holly wood in a parquetry pattern that echoes the design on the cellar floor. Limestone squares with cut corners and cocoa-colored cabochon accents add warmth and a subtle pattern, deepening the richness and beauty of the room. Whaley also purchased particular antiques to punctuate the mood, such as a nineteenth-century French iron-and-bronze chandelier

OVERLEAF: Whaley commissioned hand-painted, Georgian-style side chairs with scenes depicting four English castles.

ABOVE: The lounge area provides a transitional space, warmth, and a sense of contrast. • Diamond bins chosen for their shape line the room like paneling.

OPPOSITE: The room's centerpiece is the eighteenth-century-style French walnut tasting table. The inlaid planks of contrasting holly wood in a parquet pattern echo the cellar floor's design.

the designer found on a buying trip in Atlanta and had wired for electricity.

Further alluding to his clients' time spent in the English countryside, Whaley commissioned Georgian-style side chairs. These are hand-painted with scenes depicting four English castles that have particular meaning for the couple: Hever Castle, home to Anne Boleyn, and known for its beautiful gardens; Windsor Castle, one of the royal residences, which is located near where the clients had stayed in Surrey; the Tower of London, where the Crown Jewels are housed, and where kings stayed the night prior to their ordination; and Fountains Abbey, a ghostly ruin in the countryside that the clients found to be hauntingly romantic.

Whaley also handled the actual racking choices and wine-related elements. When the cellar reaches capacity, it will hold 2,100 bottles, stored mostly in diamond bins of French oak. The bins were chosen for their shape—the way they play off the room's geometry. Like paneling, they

line the room. The interior temperature, of course, is a chilly 56 degrees, so as much as the couple adores those chairs—their favorite element of the room—the time spent sitting on them is brief. Instead, they take a quick sip, make the wine decision, then move out to a warmer lounge area, which provides a terrific transitional space and contrast.

Outside the cellar, the vaulted ceilings descend to a more human height, which makes the space feel cozy and clubby and gives it a sense of elegant rusticity. The look is helped along by the choice of red Venetian plaster walls with flecks of gold leaf mixed into the paint. While the couple has a way to go before obsessively comparing tasting notes with fellow wine geeks, they now have an inspiring place to imbibe and share one of life's great pleasures with friends.

ABOVE, LEFT TO RIGHT: The nineteenth-century French iron-and-bronze chandelier, found by the designer on a buying trip in Atlanta, further enhances the period feel. • When the cellar reaches capacity, it will hold 2,100 bottles, stored mostly in diamond bins of French oak. • A sink, Sub-Zero refrigerator, and Riedel glassware are placed elegantly in the lounge area.

OPPOSITE: Limestone squares with cut corners and cocoa-colored cabochon accents add warmth and a subtle pattern, deepening the richness of the room.

{PART IV}

THE
MODERNIST
REFUGE

With dazzling, clever installations, contemporary materials, and highly stylized looks, the designs of the Modernist wine cellars mark a clear departure from traditional storage spaces. As with the Entertainers' cellars, they break the mold. But these spaces, which are often private, use innovative, show-offy materials that truly reflect the owners' personal design style.

In these installations, practical solutions dovetail with attitude: racking systems, cooling systems, tasting areas, and entryways all provide constant visual interest. The details make the difference in these Deco cellars, sculptural glass-and-steel cool cellars, even museumlike spaces. Modern cellars are popular in all areas of the country, from New York to California to Las Vegas, home of the cellar that most audibly articulates the aesthetic tenets of Modernist design within these pages. The interiors play with light, form, and even surprising materials to thoughtfully articulate their homeowners' aesthetic of modernist design.

L'INSTANT
TAITTINGER

DIVINE ART DECO

SAN FRANCISCO, CALIFORNIA

THE EDWARDSES WERE MORE THAN READY TO MOVE OUT OF THEIR SAN FRANCISCO APARTMENT, where too many unprotected bottles, snug in their wine racks, stretched down the long hallway. "We buy the bulk of our wine at wineries when we're in our second home in Sonoma. I keep my eye out for stuff you can't find anywhere else, the wines that float under the public radar. We wanted a wine cellar so we could age them properly and safely. Without a place to store them we were reluctant to really indulge in acquisition," said Dave Edwards, a mid-forties investment executive. So they added a new stress to their house search: "Other people need a garage or a garden; we told our Realtor if the house didn't have space for a wine cellar, don't waste our time."

The Edwardses found a 1949 charmer in the Presidio neighborhood of Sea Cliff. Its style suggested California bungalow crossed with Levittown split-level. Most importantly, it met their cellar requirement, and as a plus it came with a killer view of the Golden Gate Bridge.

The adjacent home theater had a Deco theme. Lee Zinser, their wine-cellar designer, decided to riff off of this style because the Edwardses were seeking a design

and construction that telegraphed graceful glamour. The room has a rich feel, a wonderful blend of female and male energy, like a 1930s Italian lingerie store that also sells elegant men's haberdashery. One almost expects the shopkeeper to come out and assist.

Details add the spice to the cellar. One example is the eye-catching bronze-and-glass door designed and crafted by Marilyn Kuksht, a sculptor friend of the couple's. Edwards adds, "It was fabricated by Dave Holsenbeck at a company called 'Reification'; they have quite a portfolio, including the impressive metalwork on San Francisco City Hall." The ironwork fans out over the glass like a palm leaf in a Deco style; when the door opens, the wine experience begins.

The room unfolds in a "T" shape, a long rectangle with a little tasting square at the very end of all the flash, under the shadow of the image of Catherine Deneuve voguing in a Champagne flute. The cellar shimmers, glinty with light reflecting almost everywhere. High-tone cinnamon wood plays off extraordinary coppery tiles—Italian ceramic tile with a metallic finish on the floors, and a mosaic version of the same tile on the back walls. The look is clean and modern. On one

The cellar was inspired by the adjacent home theater's Deco theme.

Marilyn Kuksht, whose projects include the impressive metal-work on San Francisco City Hall, designed and crafted the striking bronze-and-glass door.

PRESTON

Plaisir des yeux

Préparation mentale

Verser lentement

side of the highly polished woodwork some bottles lie horizontally, lined up with the wood grain, looking unexpected and elegant. On the other side of the cellar, bottles are stacked more conventionally, and the contrast works. The ceiling is quite high, and Edwards needs a stool to reach the top shelves. "I have one stool shaped like a Champagne cork," he says. "I'm not sure it fits with the rest of the style, but it's fun, and of course it fits in with the Champagne theme," he adds. Then he pauses and adds a little sheepishy, "It was a gift."

By now the Edwardses' friends have certainly discovered the couple's Champagne lust, which renders gift-giving simple. "Our friends might be afraid to give us Champagne,

PAGE 168: The room is a long rectangle of storage racks with a little tasting square at the end. The back wall boasts the classic Taittinger poster of Catherine Deneuve.

ABOVE: The storage area in the front of the cellar is separated from the small tasting area in the back by a support beam that was previously considered an eyesore. • To accentuate the high-tone cinnamon wood, the Edwardses installed copper-colored Italian ceramic tiles, a metallic finish on the floors, and a mosaic for the back walls.

OPPOSITE, CLOCKWISE FROM TOP LEFT: Silver wine pours adorn the tasting area. • The chandelier reinforces the Art Deco decor. • The entry's ironwork echoes the clean lines and shape of the period. • To discourage people from knocking into the art or the need to be straightening frames, designer Zinser embedded the prints into the burnished American cherry millwork.

but they often give us sets of flutes, which we never have enough of. And then there are the assorted finds, such as the funny stool."

Carrie Edwards's obsession with Champagne—and the bulky, irregularly shaped bottles it comes in—posed other issues that demanded attention. With about a tenth of the cellar devoted to bubbly, Zinser had to take the random sizes of the bottles into account as he envisioned the racking: "Way too often I've seen wine-cellar builders forget about the shape and weight of bottles and have to correct for it later." For this reason there's an assortment of stacks—angled, horizontal, and sideways. The couple also felt strongly about having gallery space for certain pieces of art. The huge

Catherine Deneuve Taittinger poster had to be hung, as well as vintage prints telling a narrative of wine-tasting. Zinser wanted to avoid the risk of people knocking into the pieces or the need for the Edwardses to be constantly straightening frames, so he embedded the prints into the burnished American-cherry millwork.

Accommodating art and Champagne was merely Wine Cellar–Building 101. The biggest design challenge was the unsightly structural element that a large beam imposed on the space: "Lee and I were trying to figure out if we could move it. Get rid of it. Haul it out. That's when the contractor intervened, rather strongly, saying, 'I don't think so!' Turns out the darned thing holds up the house. So Lee used the

ABOVE: The Deco narrative continues with other choices of art displayed. On one side of the highly polished woodwork, some bottles lie horizontally, lined up with the wood grain, looking unexpected and elegant.

OPPOSITE: "Way too often I've seen wine-cellar builders forget about the shape and weight of bottles and have to correct for it later," says the designer. For this reason he used an assortment of stacks—angled, horizontal, and sideways.

beam organically, separating the storage area in the front from the small tasting area in the back, where we have countertop and stemware storage. That little cubicle gets used quite often. There's something snug about sipping there under the gaze of Deneuve.

Carrie and Dave Edwards derive their greatest thrill from the way the cellar marries wine and art. The owners love the dance this juxtaposition creates, yet another way to blend the feminine and masculine. Edwards was more than happy to sacrifice some storage room to accommodate their passion for art. "Yes, for sure there is loss of space, but with two thousand bottles, Carrie and I have more wine than we can consume in a lifetime. It's worth the loss to incorporate the art."

This is San Francisco, and so when asked about having earthquake insurance, Edwards says of course they do. He then adds, "Do you know what I have that is really terrific? Have you ever heard of an accidental drinkage policy? I am totally covered for all sorts of disasters. For example, if I have a party and instead of pulling out the Bollinger non-vintage they pull out the Salon 1996, I'm covered. Now that's insurance!"

CELLAR SNAPSHOT

CAPACITY: 2,000 BOTTLES

ROEDERER ESTATE L'HERMITAGE 1999

COMTE DE LA ROCHEFOUCAULD PREMIER CRU BRUT 2002

SCHRAMSBERG J. SCHRAM 2000

SCHRAMSBERG RESERVE BRUT 1996–2001

TAITTINGER DOMAINE CARNEROS LA REVE 2001 & 2002

THE ISLAND CELLAR

NANTUCKET, MASSACHUSETTS

AS A SELF-PROCLAIMED WINE DRINKER WHO STARTED OUT ON NONDESCRIPT CHARDONNAY, JOE DONELAN, an executive at a paper-distribution company and a majority owner of Pax Wine Cellars in Sonoma, moved on not to the harder stuff, but to the better stuff.

After studying civilization in his college days and concluding that wine was history in a glass, he finally decided to get serious in 1990. That's when he struck a deal with a Nantucket sommelier for tutelage. "The deal was that I'd pay him the equivalent of a few bottles of wine and he'd create nightly tastings for my wife, Chris, and me." This led to a wine obsession and eventually to a twelve-thousand-bottle collection spread around their various domiciles. The couple has some storage in California and a four-thousand-bottle cellar in their house in Darien, Connecticut. With two cellar designs behind them by the time they began to plan for their newest home on Nantucket, Chris had something particular to say about the design: "No wood. Please. It's just so boring."

Together the couple readily rejected what they saw as ubiquitous wood-racking. They toyed with the idea of metal, thinking it might fit in seamlessly with the minimalist attitude of the house. Then Chris got excited about brick after seeing some terrific examples in a Belgian design book. But when a friend sent her a brochure of the industrially named yet ultra-sexy system called VR Professionnel, she knew she was on to something. This system is the luxe limestone shelving unit that wine-cellar designer Dionysi Grevenitis imports from Europe and installs.

Grevenitis, who has installed VP Professional in a range of projects from corporate to residential, said this kind of limestone is extremely versatile: "It moves from medieval to modern in a flash." What made the decision even sweeter was that the limestone cubbyholes are often found in the naturally cold and deep cellars of Burgundy and the Rhône, two of the Donelans' favorite wine regions. Incorporating an ancient aesthetic beneath their loft-like, airy beach house sounded like a splendid idea.

To get to the below-grade cellar, one walks down the main staircase, from the open living space, into a treasure box. Behind the plainly painted door a trio of windows shows off the collection. The Donelans stole

this inspiration from their last dinner at Thomas Keller's renowned Napa Valley restaurant, The French Laundry. There, Chris recalls seeing a window embedded in the restaurant's stone wall, affording a direct view of the cellar. "It was just beautiful," she remembers. So, too, is it here.

Joe finds the room exceedingly cozy, which is not exactly what you'd expect from a space dominated by stone. "It's absolutely the most intimate cellar I've had. Compared to the rest of the house, the cellar is a little darker, but the limestone is very warming."

More than that, he finds the limestone can transport him to Europe. "If I had poured down gravel for the floor, I'd swear I was in France." He considered using gravel, but as

OVERLEAF: The limestone cubbyholes with arched tops cradle 3,000 bottles. The racks are accented with wood.

ABOVE LEFT TO RIGHT: The entry to the cellar reflects the serene, loftlike space that exemplifies this Nantucket home. • Inspired by the designs from Thomas Keller's The French Laundry, the Donelans installed a trio of windows that show off the collection. • Donelan firmly believes in sharing wine with his family, even the good stuff.

OPPOSITE: Donelan's vineyard, Pax Wine Cellars.

the proper humidity couldn't be guaranteed, he went with the cool slate instead.

Other design details remind the visitor that this is not the Old World, with mold-covered walls, but a fabulous home at the beach. The long, narrow rectangle is slathered in a taupe-purple paint, allowing the limestone cubbyholes to shine. Three thousand bottles rest within them under their handsome, pizza oven–like arched tops. As lovely as it is, any one material is bound to get monotonous. To avoid this pitfall, Grevenitis allowed for pauses and breaks in the sections. He accented the lines and the stone with, yes, wood. In the main house are many reclaimed old beams from a dismantled Ohio factory. In the cellar, the Donelans agreed to use the wood for the countertop and to frame the stainless-steel sink, which is sunken into a split beam, adding a visual punch to the design.

On Nantucket, it is all too easy to fall into a nautical theme, a cliché the Donelans wanted to avoid. But they incorporated a few subtle references, and one more direct one. Above the sink hangs a display of rare, antique scrimshaw corkscrews, an homage to the whaling heritage of the island. The wood detail around the sink also suggests the sea. While looking for a material that would complement the old beams, Chris and Joe fell in love with mushroom wood—cypress and hemlock used in the commercial cultivation of mushrooms. Besides being a recycled material, its charm arises from the magic the mushroom's enzymes work on the wood's texture. Chris explains, "The enzymes from the mushrooms eat away at the wood, making it bumpy and very rustic. It's like natural artwork and reminds me of wood washed up on the beach."

OPPOSITE CLOCKWISE FROM TOP LEFT: For Donelan, limestone was an ideal choice for the racks. "It moves from medieval to modern in a flash." • Some of Donelan's favorite wines. • Lush details abound in the pouring area, where the wood countertop, stainless-steel sink's frame, and rare, antique scrimshaw corkscrews offer reverence to the island.

CELLAR SNAPSHOT

CAPACITY: 3,000 BOTTLES

PAX WINES: CUVÉE MORIAH, CUVÉE KELTIE

CHARDONNAY: MARCASSIN

PINOT NOIR: DUMOL; CHÂTEAUNEUF-DU-PAPE; CHÂTEAU DE BEAUCASTEL; DOMAINE DU PÉGAU

NORTHERN RHÔNE: DOMAINE JEAN-LOUIS CHAVE HERMITAGE

DOMAINE RENÉ ROSTAING

In the end, the couple didn't categorically rule out wood; they just wanted less of it, and for that they needed it to be used only for punctuation. In fact, much of the design, from the loft-like, spare attitude in the main living space above to the ancient yet modern feel in the cellar below, relies on careful editing.

"As you get older," Joe says, "you also get more mature—or, at least, your taste does. I find that I just don't need as many things or bottles. But the ones that I want, I really want. So I trimmed down my twelve-thousand-bottle collection and as a result there are only three thousand bottles here in Nantucket." Instead of taking his bottles to the auction houses, he decided to spread the wealth around his family. "I'm the oldest of eight children. I gave a fair amount of wine to my brothers and sisters."

And of course there are the gatherings where more bottles appear than people. "Some guests can't fathom that I would put out pricey bottles for a crowd. But that's what the wine is there for, to spread the gospel. On July fourth, for example, my kids were around, their friends, and several parents. I served Kistler. One couple came over and asked me why I was corrupting their child. At first I thought maybe their child wasn't old enough to drink, but then the parent added, 'This is good juice. Why are you sharing it with them?'

"I laughed and said, 'The same reason I'm sharing it with you! How will they learn if they don't ever drink the good stuff?'"

RIGHT: Despite initially ruling out using any wood, the Donelans conceded to incorporate wood as an accent or accessory, not as the main design element.

THE CLUB ROOM

ATHERTON, CALIFORNIA

AS A BUDDING WINE COLLECTOR, NORTH CALIFORNIA RESIDENT MIKE KWATINETZ found himself dining in the wine cellar of a luxe restaurant and loving it. He knew without a doubt that it was time to extract his four hundred bottles from a closet and launch his own very special project. "I really wanted to bring that experience home. I wanted to be surrounded by bottles when I was dining with my wife or with my friends. I just knew it would be terrific."

To execute that vision, Kwatinetz hired Thomas Warner Wine Cellars in Sausalito, a company that specializes in custom, hand-built cellars made from reclaimed wood. The first priority, however, was to make a space for a collection that would continue to grow. Kwatinetz explains, "Obviously my four hundred bottles were not enough. The closet they were stored in was soon going to be inadequate." It didn't take long to get his collection up to speed, thanks to a buying frenzy fed by trips to Italy, France, and Australia, not to mention the yearly trip to Napa that his firm has taken for the last nine years. "It started to get out of control," he remembers.

The problem was that the Kwatinetzes' house had no basement in which to install a cellar, so Mike and Michelle decided to build one. "It was a very complicated job," Kwatinetz says. "We had to dig under the house; they had to add house supports. It took about a year to complete after we broke ground."

Tom Warner's design responded to Kwatinetz's desire for high ceilings and a cellar that would reflect his sense of strict order, while delivering the sense of visual drama that starts with a Murano-glass statue of a woman set in an arch, as if to beckon, *This way*. "Depending on how we light the cellar, it may be the only thing illuminated," Kwatinez says. But that kind of flourish is limited to the foyer, because Kwatinetz wanted a very clean, or as he put it, "tucked-in" look for the cellar.

The whole space is extremely tucked in, and quite literally contains a room tucked into another, a room-within-a-room. Around the perimeter of the room is the wine cellar. Safe behind floor-to-ceiling glass, inside the temperature-controlled space, are the approximately two thousand bottles. A black granite countertop running the length of the back wall is polished to a glossy, reflective sheen. Mirrors bounce the light off the interiors. The effect is highly reflective—so much so that when sitting at a more comfortable temperature in the room, it is a very clubby affair. The room resembles a 1920s hotel card room filled with cigar-smoking men, with its round tables with caned chairs. Kwatinetz remarks, "No matter which way you look, you see the cellar. You're surrounded by bottles." Of course, that was what he was after all along.

With all the bottles, the effect could have been dizzying. Kwatinetz was careful to keep a clean look in the cellar, behind the glass, and provide a separate storage area for boxes. "I didn't want crates piled up, so we built shelves that can be adjusted to accommodate any size crate. It's all very uniform, very neat," he says. In fact, it is so neat that the challenge for Warner was to keep the space from looking *too* cold. "The right woods help immensely." Warner advocated for lots of mahogany, the Zelig of woods. "It can change and absorb color beautifully and the stain we chose brings out the warm honey color of the wood; it's just spectacular."

Instead of the more common wine-bin slats, the arches were built out of solid wood—a luxe choice that resulted in a very finished, elegant look. "Sometimes I view my work as creating elaborate picture frames for artwork,"

OVERLEAF: The Kwatinetz cellar is a dramatic room-within-a-room.

RIGHT: To keep the space from looking too cold, Warner chose to use mahogany in a honey-hued stain. Says Warner, "It can change and absorb color beautifully, and the stain we chose brings out the warm honey color of the wood; it's just spectacular."

OPPOSITE: For designer Tom Warner, a wine cellar is like theatre. In fact, in this case, it is dinner theatre with a twist. Kwatinetz is the owner, the sommelier, and the diner.

says Warner. "The wine bottle is the art. For instance, in one of the arches, Mike has a bottle of 1945 d'Yquem. Now, this is a sweet wine, and as it gets older, it takes on a darker color—it can be almost like maple syrup when it's this old. It's a fabulous wine, a piece of art, and a piece of history. It's spectacular." On the glass shelf of another arch sits a '58 Port; on another, a Czech crystal vase.

Lighting plays a key role in the environment and segues from a warm, burnt-umber glow from cove lighting in the high ceiling in the tasting room to the dramatic, direct highlights of the track lighting that's trained on the wine shelves. "We put in a lot of different lighting so that we'd have a lot of illuminative choices. We can highlight the

ABOVE: Reflective materials abound to enhance the thoughtful lighting design—molding, mirrors, and goldleaf add another dimension.

display bottles, but we also have lighting around the edge of the glass and racks, plus cove lighting, center lighting—all on dimmers," says Kwatinetz. The biggest challenge, however, was how to spotlight the glass shelves in the arches to avoid bouncing a glare around. By playing with the depth of the light recesses, they were able to position the lights so that they spread a soft glow that bathes rather than burns the highlighted objects.

Warner points out that a wine cellar is like theatre. In fact, in this case, it is dinner theatre with a twist. Kwatinetz is the owner, the sommelier, and the diner. His mind even works like a sommelier's: "What I like about collecting and having a cellar is thinking about what I want to buy. I like to consider

what's a great wine for a fair price," he says. "For me, the contemplation is as much fun as the drinking, in some ways." Yet he's also an appreciative guest in his own space. "Just having a glass of wine, some hors d'oeuvres down there—it somehow tastes better with the right ambience."

ABOVE: The focal point of the cellar is a Murano glass statue of a woman under an arch. "Depending on how we light the cellar, it may be the only thing illuminated," Kwatinetz says.

ABOVE RIGHT: A black granite countertop running the length of the back wall, polished to a glossy, reflective sheen, complements extraordinary wines such as this 1945 d'Yquem.

CELLAR SNAPSHOT

CAPACITY: 2,000 BOTTLES
1997 PETER MICHAEL CABERNET
1997 PHELPS INSIGNIA CABERNET
1997 CAYMUS CABERNET
1996 PENFOLD GRANGE
2001 HARLAN
1998 HAUT-BRION
2004 ROBERT MONDAVI OAKVILLE CABERNET
2004 TURLEY ZINFINDELS
2004 PETER MICHAEL BELLE COTE CHARDONNAY
DESSERT WINES: 2001 CHÂTEAU SUDUIRAUT
1990 D'YQUEM

AGE OF ANTIQUITY

BROOKLYN, NEW YORK

WHILE DINING ALFRESCO ON THE COMPELLING AMALFI COAST OF ITALY, SOMETHING CLICKED FOR THIS Brooklyn mother of six. "'So that's what all of this is about,' I said to myself. Right then I understood what had in the past eluded me: Sitting down with family and friends over long meals with good food and a great glass of wine is one of the important joys of life. I wanted to bring that into my house." The trouble was, Maggie and her husband have a strict kosher home and until recently, finding enough kosher wines to fill a wine cellar was a Herculean task.

As if that weren't enough, she still needed to sell her husband on the idea. "He thought I was crazy. Now," she says, laughing, "he takes all the credit."

The couple started to learn and to ferret out the wines available. They traveled, shopped, and inquired. He sought out cellar-worthy kosher wines and discovered Covenant, a boutique Napa Cabernet, as well as Domaine du Castel, a Bordeaux-style red from one of the first, and best, *garagiste* producers in Israel.

Recently, they visited Hagafen in Napa, netting cases of its hard-to-find, high-end microcuvee Prix Cabernet Sauvignon. When they determined that they could fill up the shelves, they decided on a one-thousand-bottle-capacity storage area, styled with plenty of pizzazz.

With a background in archaeology and anthropology, Maggie has a great attachment to all things ancient. She immediately connected with Brooklyn-based designer Dionysi Grevenitis of Dalst Stone Wine Cellars, who came onboard to build a museum-worthy mise-en-scène for her at the bottom of the mahogany spiral staircase that links her library to her tasting room. The journey begins at the stunning three-hundred-year-old Turkish amphorae that guard the tasting area like sentries. Grevenitis wanted an arched and dramatic doorway into the actual cellar because he wanted to give Maggie the feeling of walking under King David's Gate in Jerusalem.

One material choice helped achieve the goal: travertine stone, which became the guiding theme of the cellar. Maggie said that when she initially saw the sedimentary stone in a melding of beige, cream, and pink tones, she almost felt plunked down a few thousand years ago in the Mediterranean. She was so taken with it that she also used it to floor her 6,000-square-foot Federal-style mansion.

While the flooring was now settled, the wine-racking was another process. Maggie had definite opinions about what she did not want: "I find wood so claustrophobic." As she flatly refused to even consider any kind of wooden shelving, she was thrilled to find a near-at-hand solution. Grevenitis's line of Dalst Stone Wine Cellars racks are made of limestone from the Comblanchien quarries in Burgundy's Côte de Nuits; the elegantly spare, heavy stone wine-racking can be found in top wineries such as Dujac in Burgundy, Latour in Bordeaux, and Veuve Clicquot in Champagne. It seemed perfect for this project. The hand-hewn feel of Dalst's system dovetailed seamlessly with the modern/ancient yin-yang of

her house. The bins look clean, sleek—more airy and open than the traditional wooden grid, and very sophisticated, in a creamy taupe hue.

Grevenitis and his partner, Theodore Finkle, only began importing the Dalst racks in 2005, not long before the plans for this house and wine cellar began to coalesce. "My wife is from Alsace so we go to France a lot, and I kept seeing this stone system there," Grevenitis explains. "It's nothing like wood, a low-grade insulator. The only thing wood has going for it in a wine cellar is that it cradles the bottles; you don't have to worry about clanging them."

Ferra Designs, a Brooklyn-based company specializing in

OVERLEAF: The doorway design is meant to evoke the feeling of crossing King David's Gate in Jerusalem.

ABOVE: Beneath the spiral staircase, 300-year-old Turkish amphorae flank the tasting room. Dionysi Grevenitis of Dalst Stone Wine

Cellars created a cellar that pays homage to his client's background in archaeology and anthropology.

OPPOSITE: Black steel corner shelving enhances the stone's clean lines and the cellar's high ceilings.

hand-forged metalwork, was enlisted to build the set of massive, double-paned glass doors. The idea was that they would be framed in a minimum of metal but accented with a pair of sensuously heavy, undulating steel handles that seem to float in the air. The entrance is so grand that the petite room (narrow enough that you can almost touch all of the shell-pink walls if you stand in its center) comes as a bit of a shock. Yet instead of being claustrophobic, the very quality Maggie wanted to avoid, the 9-foot ceilings and museum-quality lighting imbue the space with a feeling of freedom and expansiveness.

Grevenitis suggested painting the walls behind the shelving Pompeii red to set off the pink stone and give the room a sultry look. The color choice also created a sense of continuity with the rest of the house: With Samuel Botero designing the interior, the bright and bold are essential aethestics for the overall design.

Ferra's metal touches appear throughout. Black steel corner shelving accents the clean lines of the stone, as well as the cellar's height. That height presented a challenge. As the cellar was a late addition to the house's plans, most of the HVAC had been run. Grevenitis had to find another solution for hiding the air-control ducting for the cellar. Grevenitis explains, "I couldn't use a ducted split system like I would have if I'd had the use of the ceiling." Instead, he hid the system in a pillar; the only sign that there's machinery within is a demure bronze grate about a foot off the floor. "Then I trenched out part of the floor, and put a bronze grate over it.

ABOVE LEFT TO RIGHT: The double-paned glass doors were designed by Ferra Designs, a Brooklyn-based company specializing in hand-forged metalwork. The interior of the limestone racks is subtly lit to illuminate the bottles.

I run the warm water from the cooling system into the trench, where it drains out." Not only does it work from a design perspective, but it also contributes to the humidity in the room—furthering the self-sustaining nature of a stone cellar.

While most people think of connecting their cellar to their kitchen or dining room, Maggie had another purpose in mind. Up those spiraling stairs rests her aerie of a library—an extensive cache of historical fiction, history, and archaeology books—suspended on a balcony overlooking that black-marble floor. As in the cellar, she says, "The look is very cool, but warm at the same time. And it's a very tranquil retreat. I felt that that's what a library should be—a retreat, some-place you can relax and unwind after dinner. And what really could be better than curling up in the corner with a good book and a glass of wine?"

CELLAR SNAPSHOT

CAPACITY: 1,000 BOTTLES
COVENANT
DOMAINE DU CASTEL
HAGAFEN

LEFT: Spiral stairs connect the cellar to the library. "And what really could be better than curling up in the corner with a good book and a glass of wine?" Maggie says.

ABOVE: Maggie wanted her 1,000-bottle cellar to be a conversation piece in its own right.

OPPOSITE, CLOCKWISE FROM TOP LEFT: The travertine stone transports the visitor to the Mediterranean of two millennia ago. • Metal sconces add modernity to the space and skillfully contrast with the travertine and limestone. • Adding to the elegance of the space is thoughtful, museum-quality lighting. • The limestone wine racks are sourced from the Comblanchien quarries in Burgundy's Côte de Nuits.

KOSHER WINE

(BASED ON AN INTERVIEW WITH THOMAS K. METHANS, A WINE PORTFOLIO CONSULTANT BASED IN BROOKLYN)

Kosher wine has changed markedly over last twenty years. Because of the wine's reputation of poor quality and worse flavor, a wine store might have stocked a few inexpensive kosher varieties at best. These days the kosher landscape has certainly improved. Wineries are catching up with contemporary tastes and are practicing better fruit selection and modernized wine-making techniques. This is wonderful news for wine collectors: They have the advantage of greater selection, access, and availability of fine wines at a wider range of prices. Previously, most kosher wines were inexpensive and utilitarian, and it was often difficult to find a really good bottle no matter how much you wanted to spend.

For everyday drinking, there is a variety of kosher wines from around the world: Europe, South America, Australia, the United States, and of course Israel. For the high-end options, rely on prime wine regions in California and classically expensive areas such as Champagne, Bordeaux, and Burgundy. There are more than two hundred high-quality labels available.

WHAT IS A KOSHER WINE?

Kosher wine must be created, bottled, opened, handled, and poured only by Jews. There is one exception. If the wine is heated to near boiling, it can be handled by non-Jews. These wines are called "mevushal."

BETTER FLAVOR THROUGH BETTER WINE-MAKING:

Some kosher products have improved in flavor simply because kosher wineries hired outside winemakers and consultants.

BETTER FLAVOR THROUGH MODERN TECHNOLOGY:

To avoid unpleasant-tasting cooked wine, wineries can now employ "flash pasteurization" to preserve a wine's flavor and integrity. In order to be mevushal, wine is heated to about 185° Fahrenheit for about fifteen to thirty seconds and then cooled immediately. Almost every processed liquid goes through these steps: fruit juice, milk, high-production beers, and any other perishable liquid that needs to sit on a shelf.

THOMAS K. METHANS, PORTFOLIO CONSULTANT AT SIP FINE WINE IN BROOKLYN, NEW YORK, RECOMMENDS THE FOLLOWING KOSHER WINES:

BUBBLY:
Laurent Perrier
  (Champagne)
Bartenura Prosecco (Italy)
Pommery (Champagne)

WHITES:
Pascal Bouchard
  (Burgundy)

Goose Bay (New Zealand)
Barkan (Israel)

REDS:
Covenant (California)
Baron de Rothschild
  (Bordeaux)
Noah Winery (Israel)
Fechas de Los Andes

(Argentina)
Capcanes, Peraj Petita
  (Spain)

DESSERT:
Queen Esther (Israel)
Ramparts de Baster
  (Sauternes)
Herzog (California)

VEGAS DELIGHT

LAS VEGAS, NEVADA

WHEN THIS SUCCESSFUL FORTYSOMETHING REAL-ESTATE EXECUTIVE ENVISIONED A TROPHY HOME FOR HIS FAMILY in the booming and trendy section of Las Vegas, Red Rock, he was adamant: As far as his wine storage went, he wanted an artistic statement consistent with his home's distinctive aesthetics. From the start he wanted his house, as well as his wine display, to be a functional piece of art.

In order that every detail could be attended to, the ten-thousand-square-foot house took almost six years to complete. The setting and atmosphere had to be spot-on for fantastic entertaining and also serve as a fantasy playground for the couple's twins. Everything, from the Gehry-inspired twisty-turny, hyperbolic paraboloid roof, to the Karen Butera interiors, was to be show-stopping. And even though the couple was new to the subtleties of the wine world, so new in fact that they were more into boutique beers and perfect cocktails than Clos de Bèze, they viewed a wine cellar as a luxury amenity and a design opportunity. Even though their plans included a distinctive focal point in the bar, they set aside some prime dining-room footage for their small but growing wine collection. The wine cellar would be part of the dining room's compelling visual and dramatic scale. They wanted some bottle splash.

Their wine storage designer was Ben Benoit of the Los Angeles–based Cellar Masters, who had segued from stage director to wine-cellar builder/guru in 1990. He remembers that the client wanted something visually different.

Benoit's Cellar Masters *is* different. Holding both contracting and air-conditioning licenses, they build everything from wood supports to wire items in their shops. No "off-the-rack" racking for their clients. "To further charge the spirit of their cellars," Benoit adds, "all of our principals are winos and wine nuts."

Obviously "different" still had to mesh with the rest of the disciplined contemporary aesthetic the owners' designer, Karen Butera, spread throughout the house, from river pebbles and leather walls in the powder room to plenty of stainless-steel detailing, African mahogany, and flowing glass in the living areas. Exposed to the extravagant examples that grace the restaurants ensconced in grand Las Vegas hotels, the couple was looking for something similar—a wine cellar that acted as an art piece.

Benoit recalls, "The beginning was a roller coaster when it came to materials. This is the most modern design we have executed. It had to be; because the house uses clean details we needed to keep in step. We started with stainless steel and that led to Lucite panels and then it morphed into illuminated Lucite with wrought-iron bottle supports."

But before they progressed to the gorgeous detail, a huge problem had to be solved: integrating the temperature control into the house's aesthetic. Benoit said that this presented the most difficult cooling control project he's yet encountered. "Las Vegas is the desert. It's hot. And to exaggerate the problems, the wine display was to be situated in the open dining area, enclosed with glass walls, and on top of it all, a twenty-eight-foot-high glass transom."

While the technology exists to square away this concern, hiding the awkward equipment was another issue altogether. If the design of the house had been industrial

OVERLEAF: The wine cellar is an integral element in the dining room's dramatic mod appeal.

ABOVE LEFT TO RIGHT: Despite the cellar's petite size—500–600 bottles—its effects are hypnotizing to visitors. • The cellar's magic is created with illuminated Lucite and wrought-iron bottle supports.

OPPOSITE: Despite the enormity of the house, Benoit was given a wine closet with available depth of only 18 inches.

modern, that would have been fine, but for refined contemporary, exposed pipes and wires just would not suit.

No stranger to imaginative thinking, Benoit had to put his imagination into overdrive for this project. "When the client heard our first idea, to expose the cooling system, they got nervous, and we realized that we had to figure out a more eye-appealing solution."

A loft-like office is perched directly above the 80-inch-long wine wall. The trick was to hide the custom ducting system, but where? "Our solution was to claim the existing joist above the storage area and then we created a soffit to hide all the stuff."

Even though the house is spacious, the depth for this wine closet was limited to a mere 18 inches. The cellar was not going to be huge, but it would be quite adequate for the homeowners' needs, which were in the five-to-six-hundred-bottle range. Considering that the average bottle is 11½ inches tall, space usage needed to be inventive. To make it work, Benoit chose slimmer metal racking. The racking was then angled with wrought-iron hinges, so bottles could fit triple-deep. When the rack is filled up, the wires give the illusion of floating, gravity-defying bottles.

The clients wanted that visual "pop" and they got it. Butera defined the artistic details of the wine display. "The couple," Butera says, "is committed to consistent disciplined design throughout the house. They love that existing materials are repeated and the same green-quartzite slate, custom-fabricated in a harlequin pattern in the dining room, continues into the wine wall. It's important to keep elements like that in flow."

Fueled by the Butera design, Benoit riffed accordingly by creating dividing panels of Lucite with stainless steel. Inside the panels he used frosted acrylic, infused from the back with blue LED lights, which creates a blue frost. The dividing panels are 4½ inches of column. And to seal it all in, he opted for ½-inch insulated glass doors that keep the air in tight.

"Technologically it looks simple, but it's complex," Benoit said. "And I'm really pleased with it all."

OPPOSITE: The blue frost is created by illuminating the backs of frosted acrylic panels with blue LED lights.

ABOVE: Taking cues from local restaurants, the couple wanted their wine cellar to be an art piece.

PART V

URBAN RETREATS
AND INSPIRING
SPACES:
BEYOND THE HOME WINE CELLAR

Overcoming challenges often sparks tremendous creativity, and the urban wine cellar reflects this. Oenophiles who don't have a chateau-sized space can still create fantastic homes for their wines. Few people know this better than urban collectors, who have to reconcile their big appetites for wine with limited square footage. Savvy solutions are also ideal for wine lovers who are just beginning to gather a critical mass of wine. The goal is to make the most of the space available in order to artfully display and organize the budding collection.

Underlining the close relationship between residential and commercial design, the country's newest and award-winning commercial wine cellars, located anywhere from restaurants and hotels to private clubs, offer inspiration that has already begun to influence the way wine collectors think about their home cellars. And, of course, they offer the truly passionate and the merely wine-curious more opportunities than ever to extend their enjoyment of the good grape outside their own four walls.

CHELSEA GIRL

NEW YORK, NEW YORK

A FLIRTATIOUS MEAL IN PARIS COUPLED WITH A LUSCIOUS ST. EMILION FUELED THIS YOUNG woman's wine-foraging rampage. She started out cautiously with a few bottles, but by the time she acquired her Chelsea loft space, she knew her collection was going to multiply. The growing assortment of bottles was fated to be problematic if she didn't find a way to handle it.

All the other collectors she knew in New York stored their wine in off-site facilities, or in one of those noisy wine refrigerators. Those solutions would not work for her. So even though she lived in the kind of city where the sale of a firstborn for more square footage is a common joke, she decided she would make the ultimate sacrifice . . . specifically a 30-inch by 52-inch chunk of her apartment. Hiding her "cellar" behind a windowless door, her architect, Rene Gonzalez, followed a theme of the entire living space: You never know what lurks behind the door.

"Behind every door or panel is a surprise," says Miami architect Gonzalez. "Everything is folded away, hidden. Even the kitchen and the guest bed are hidden. We wanted to maintain the openness of the loft while keeping the important living detail hidden. The result is discovery and magic. For example, when the door off of the foyer is opened," Gonzalez says, "instead of a coat closet you are confronted by this very rich cellar made out of mahogany and slate. The materials contrast with the exterior and the clean lines and minimalist appeal of the apartment, and that's what gives the sense of discovery and a sense of 'Aha!'"

Bigger than a bread box but no smaller than a luxurious shower stall, this wine cellar can handle up to eight hundred bottles. It is a stretched rectangle, a tiny bit over 10 feet high, with virtually floor-to-ceiling racking.

The client had a yearning to line the walls with bronze-colored slate. Her choice suited Gonzalez very well, as he had already envisioned using traditional materials—dark, rich, and warm. In addition to loving the understated quality of bronze, she adores the fact that the room is hidden, as if she were sitting on a secret. "When the door opens and guests look at it, their reaction is inevitably 'Wow!'" she says.

Another feature she is fond of is the functionality of the space. Selecting wine from it is easy, because its size

and extra shelving afford surfaces for glasses and wine paraphernalia. Once the guests admire the cellar, they can easily choose their stemware from her eclectic mix of options. "They are intentionally mismatched, the result of requesting them over the years as gifts for Christmas or birthdays. The idea is to have everyone at a dinner party pick his or her favorite. It gives an individuality to the table and eliminates the which-glass-is-mine confusion!"

While her cellar is currently only half-full she is beginning her palate formation and wine acquisition, and she knows it won't be long before it bulges to capacity. As a woman who helps businesses go green, she is very definitely the face of a new breed of collector, one who leans heavily on

OVERLEAF: This Chelsea girl reclaimed a 30" x 52" space to build a special wine closet designed by architect Rene Gonzalez.

ABOVE LEFT TO RIGHT: The racks, bottles, slate, and bright colors inside the cellar mark a departure from the clean lines of the apartment.

salespeoples' recommendations and not on the well-known critics and the scores they give. In fact, her favorite way to buy is on the road. She says, "I love to bring back wine from trips, as I did when I visited Argentina and South Africa. The usual plan is to buy six bottles and then we drink one bottle a year, to watch the progression in the wine's evolution."

"Obviously, I started out as a Bordeaux lover and I still am," she says, referring to her Parisian initiation to the wine world. "I absolutely have my favorites, like Mission Haut-Brion. But on the whole what I am looking for is the adventure." She reflects, "When it comes to buying, I deal with wine the same way I buy art. I go through spurts. I am inconsistent and driven by emotion. I'm not after investment. I'm after inspiration."

CELLAR SNAPSHOT

CAPACITY: 2,000 BOTTLES

CHAMPAGNES:

ROEDERER ESTATE L'HERMITAGE 1999

COMTE DE LA PREMIER CRU BRUT 2002

SCHRAMSBERG J. SCHRAM 2000

SCHRAMSBERG RESERVE BRUT 1996–2001

TAITTINGER DOMAINE CARNEROS LA REVE 2001 & 2002

LEFT: "When the door off of the foyer is opened," Gonzalez says, "instead of a coat closet, you are confronted by this very rich cellar made out of mahogany and slate."

THE BACHELOR ENTHUSIAST

NEW YORK, NEW YORK

NEW YORK CITY, A LAND OF OPPORTUNITY FOR WINE DRINKING AND BUYING, also poses a great big headache for wine collectors. The problem, in one word, is "space." Naturally, there's almost never enough. For most people with serious collections, off-site storage is the only solution.

But some oenophiles refuse to be separated from their bottles. They want their collection right next to them, at their fingertips, to be able to count their bottles and drink them when they want. New York City–based designer Scott Salvator points out, "If that's the case, as it was in my client's, and you're going to take over living space for a wine cellar, it's a boon to be single so no one is going to argue with you if you want to shrink the laundry room or take away closet space for your favorite beverage."

Salvator specializes in luxury design, and while he often works on a grand scale, as in the Sherry-Netherland and the Café Carlyle, he also takes on certain precious projects, like this one on the Upper East Side of Manhattan. "The client is an important figure on the buy-and-sell market," Salvator says. "He has a collection of heavy-hitters in Rhône and Burgundy.

Among the bottles, plenty are oversized, creating a problem: how to shoehorn them into his relatively small but chic two-bedroom apartment, one that stretches from front to back?"

The room selected for takeover was a 6-foot-square closet in the middle of the long, narrow hallway. Salvator says, "Sure, the owner would love to have had more space, but any space would be too small for him. When his home in Charleston is finished, he'll have a huge wine cellar. For the time being, I am making New York City work for him."

Wine cellar designer Fred Tregaskis of New England Wine Cellars was enlisted. A wine collector himself, he noted the seriousness of this particular collection and he wanted to pay it respect. "What we needed," says Tregaskis, "was a no-nonsense, handsome design that was ultra-functional. The bottles needed easy in-and-out. The client had no problem with the grid's professional, boxy look. But that didn't mean the design couldn't be fun as well."

Tregaskis chose redwood for the double-deep racked grid, mixing in a few diamond bins for easily grabbing everyday wine. "There's not room for much in that

The homeowner co-opted a six-foot-square closet in the center of his apartment.

The maple-framed door is
flanked by two floor-to-ceiling
glass panels, displaying the
homeowner's prized bottles.

space," he says, "but no matter how small a room I'm working with, I always allow for a table or ledge. One of the terrific aspects of this, the equivalent to a wine walk-in closet, is that the owner can enter the room, his arms laden, and perch the crates on the copper table. The table is a mere twelve inches, but it gets the job done. I do love the metal for its versatility in look. Polish it and go for modern or get the patina and go for antique."

Tregaskis can always be counted on to extract great style from a space, even if, as in this case, the client's need was all about function. "The power of paint can't be denied. The color red here is very festive. This kind of room is a celebration and shouldn't be taken too, too seriously; let it be the bright spot it is."

All the men involved in the project—the client, Tregaskis, and Salvator—agree on their favorite design element: the maple-framed door flanked by two floor-to-ceiling glass door panels. These show off the bottles and also open up the hallway, saving it from feeling dark and claustrophobic. "It's colorful and cozy; the bottles are the center of attention. In fact," Tregaskis says, noting a bonus for a single man, "it's quite sexy."

PAGE 210: The cellar is comprised of a redwood double-deep racked grid, a small shelf for unpacking, and a few diamond bins for easy access.

RIGHT: "What we needed," says designer Tregaskis, "was a no-nonsense, handsome design that was ultrafunctional. The bottles needed easy in and out. The client had no problem with the grid's professional, boxy look. But that didn't mean the design couldn't be fun as well."

OPPOSITE: "The power of paint can't be denied. The color red here is very festive. This kind of room is a celebration and shouldn't be taken too, too seriously; let it be the bright spot it is," says the designer.

ZEN CLOSET

MALIBU, CALIFORNIA

"WHERE MY HUSBAND SAW AN UGLY CLOSET UNDERNEATH THE MAIN STAIRCASE, I saw a wine cellar," Nicole Sassaman says.

But that's not an unusual scenario for Sassaman. As one of Southern California's most successful TV design personalities and real estate "flippers," she is always seeing a vision when others see only an eyesore. She can thank that talent for being able to buy, remodel, and sell the Greta Garbo house for $7,500,000. Soon after that sale, she relocated to her present, beachy Malibu house and reconfigured its dreariness by adding expanses of high-polished walnut, well-distributed Buddhas, and monochromatic simplicity.

One of Sassaman's bugaboos is wasted space. To her, that closet was such an offender—but even worse, it was a design blemish that needed to be resolved, and putting in wine storage there seemed a good fit. She'd had a wine cellar in the Garbo house, and with that in mind, she started in earnest to work her transformative magic.

"The stairs were covered with horrible, putty-colored carpet. Gone. The rail was like a 1970s den. Gone. The storage space underneath was not even Home Depot's best. It had to go," she recounts with a sweep of the arm.

Few people get as thrilled by the thought of a wrecking ball. In this case, Sassaman was eager to see her vision come to life. After the staircase was demolished, she rebuilt the steps in the same shiny walnut wood that warms the house and the majority of the floors. The staircase was reconfigured with industrial materials, stainless steel, and glass. Sassman acquired a huge slab of walnut with which to support the railing as well as frame the top of the triangular cellar.

What she created is an evocative space. Treehouse? Tent? Art installation? It's hard to settle on one singular image, but the room behind the glass doors demands admiration. It also fits into the total Zen-like, calming feel of her home design. That soothing walnut flooring spreads into the cellar. Wine wraps—like stripes— around the three walls. Bottles are inserted like pegs into holes. The planking between the wines is actual shelving. Sassaman explained that she could have created a book-and-wine library within, but she preferred the empty space. Demure and petite. Ten feet long by six feet deep. A vision of minimalism. Could the project have been simpler?

"Ha!" Sassaman laughs. "There was nothing simple about it! Of course, breaking out the closet was simple. The idea of reclaiming the space for another use was simple. Anyone can do it. But my cabinetmaker has known me for a long time and has plenty of patience. He was very precise, a much-needed quality, because there was so much trouble working with all of the different angles in the room. I'm always asking him to do something crazy."

Actually, the end result proves she knew exactly what she was doing. The walnut shelving is anchored firmly into the wall. No hardware is visible. Lego-like, the long pieces of racking wood fit snugly into the supportive columns. Sassaman nods knowingly. "Simplicity takes a lot of skill to

OVERLEAF: "Where my husband saw an ugly closet underneath the main staircase, I saw a wine cellar," Nicole Sassaman says.

ABOVE, LEFT TO RIGHT: Sassaman is an experienced builder. She anchored walnut shelving firmly into the wall without any visible hardware. • There is no wasted space: Bottles are inserted like pegs into holes with planks that double as shelving.

OPPOSITE: A walnut slab supports the railing and frames the top of the triangular cellar.

pull off. Everything has to be visually perfect when the lines are this minimalistic."

When asked about temperature control, Sassaman says she decided against it. "We were lucky. The main wall sits under the soil outside and that has an insulating effect. Mostly the temperature seems to stay naturally around sixty degrees and that's perfect for my needs. Sure, I love wine, but I'm no expert. I am, however, getting more into it and beginning to think that if we start to collect age-worthy selections, we might need to be more careful about heat. Temperature control wouldn't be too hard to add."

If she develops an appetite for large-format bottles, she'll have a challenge to address, as the present bottle holes are not deep or wide enough for magnums. "But they are big enough for Champagne bottles!" she explains. The designer has some priorities!

OPPOSITE: Sassaman demolished the original staircase and replaced the steps with the same walnut that appears throughout the house and the floors.

ABOVE: The architecture of the space is calming, like the rest of the home's interiors.

Her idea for the wine cellar was more visual than anything else. The room suits her needs right this minute, by providing visual delight. "I really need things to be different," she says, referring to her unusual method of racking. "I first developed the hole-racking in the Garbo house. But I was so frustrated! That cellar was in the basement, so no one saw it. This time, I wanted to show it off, like another piece of beautiful furniture in my home. I wanted drama and I wanted it to be its own environment."

And she got her wish. "I just love looking at the cellar, which is in the sight-line from my dining room. Sitting there with friends, eating dinner, I see it as a glowing jewel box. The whole cellar in the staircase is completely unexpected. Design can change your life, or at least change your mood. I think one of my favorite things about the cellar is people's reaction to it. More often than not, it makes them smile."

RIGHT: Sassaman describes the display as "LEGO-like," with long pieces of racking wood nestled into the supportive columns.

OPPOSITE: The cellar is designed for rotating inventory and standard bottles. While Sassaman has room for Champagne, large-format bottles are too wide and deep.

CLUB PARADISE

ST. HELENA, CALIFORNIA

NOT FAR FROM THE TONY NAPA TOWN OF ST. HELENA, TUCKED INTO THE VINES AND THE BRONZE MADRONA TREES, is one of the most exclusive wine clubs around, The Napa Valley Reserve. The Reserve sprung from the imagination of H. William Harlan, owner of the über-cult winery Harlan Estate. Among the four hundred members of this club devoted to the celebration of wine, arts, and letters are the very private owners of some of the world's most prestigious wine collections. This club distinguishes itself from others by offering the opportunity for members to play wine-maker and produce their own wine from the Reserve's organic vineyards. Should they wish, they may rent a locker in the exclusive dining room beneath the winery. The storage spaces and tasting areas offer creative solutions for collectors to use in their own homes.

Because The Napa Valley Reserve is a working winery, the wine-maker absolutely insisted that no wood or natural fabrics should be used when designing the dining room which houses those individual wine lockers. Architects and designers on the job, most importantly Jesse Whitesides of A-Squared Studios and Dionysi Grevenitis of Dalst Stone Wine Cellars, use no wood or natural fabrics. While this may seem Draconian, the point is to avoid any possible material on which 2,4,6-trichloroanisole (TCA), the bacteria responsible for so-called "corked" (or tainted) wines, can grow. A microscopic amount of this, the bane of the wine world, can turn a gorgeous wine into something about as pleasant-smelling and -tasting as if you licked the walls of a moldy basement.

The team's ability to rise to the challenge of avoiding materials that would allow TCA bacteria to grow was never doubted; the only question was how to create an inviting space out of stone, metal, and plastic. Texture was the answer; it abounds in this cellar. The walls are done in a pebbled stucco, and a Dalst stone storage system was a natural choice, as the limestone it uses feels so natural in this very subterranean, cave-like setting. There are sixty bin-like lockers available for members to rent to store their personal Napa Valley Reserve wines. To make sure no one gets confused about whose bin belongs to whom, safekeeping is needed. Whitesides had individual iron doors mongered by a local craftsperson. Now each locker can be kept under lock and key. Metal also makes an

appearance in the impressive rectangular table, but this time it is warming copper, fashioned of 3-inch plate. Chilewich woven vinyl appears here as a carpet. Chairs are covered in an outdoor fabric which is used for the drapery as well, and, when needed, as a tablecloth on top of the 3-inch-plate copper dining table.

Because no one likes dining in the cold, this room is heated. The wines in residence are not terribly old, and the temperature rarely goes above 70 degrees. Since the room is about festivity, the wines the members stock here are just for the moment, so the harm is minimal.

The overall impact of the entertaining area is further enhanced by the storage area. Grevenitis loves how the stone bins interplay with their respective metal gates. Whitesides adds, "We were looking for clean and sophisticated without being too contemporary." With the stucco walls and the ironwork, the aesthetic is instant Iberia, but with Napa style.

OVERLEAF: Pebbled stucco walls and limestone bins contribute to the cavelike feeling in the exclusive dining room beneath The Napa Valley Reserve's winery, where sixty binlike lockers are available for members.

ABOVE, LEFT TO RIGHT: A copper-plated table rests on top of a Chilewich vinyl carpet. To minimize the need for natural fabrics, which can complicate the wine-making process, outdoor fabric is used for covering chairs, as drapery or, when needed, as a tablecloth. • Napa Valley members can produce their own wine from the Reserve's organic vineyards. The dining room offers opportunities to share wines and design solutions for their own cellars.

OPPOSITE, CLOCKWISE FROM TOP LEFT: TNVR boasts being one of the country's most exclusive wine clubs, with membership of 400 of the world's most passionate oenophiles. • The dining area doesn't store very old wines; the room can be heated so guests don't dine in a cold room. • Architect Whitesides enjoys the play of the stucco walls, limestone bins, and metal gates. "We were looking for clean and sophisticated without being too contemporary." • The winemaker calls the shots: No wood or natural fabrics can be used in the dining room, where there are individual wine lockers, because the Reserve is a working winery.

WRAPPED IN WINE

NEW YORK, NEW YORK

WHEN THE ESTEEMED CHEF ALAIN DUCASSE CONCEIVED OF HIS RESTAURANT, ADOUR, he knew that it was to be tucked into the St. Regis Hotel. He also knew that he wanted the interiors to pay homage to food and wine. With this in mind he went straight to the award-winning Rockwell Group for his architecture and design. This space is not just a beautiful cellar, but is also a sleek storage space for a select few city-slickers and VIPs, who stow their precious bottles of wine here—think of a very high-end concierge service—in lieu of sticking them in self-storage.

The restaurant opened in 2008 and, thanks to David Rockwell, there is no mistaking its mission. All one has to do is to glide past the gilded rococo flourishes of the St. Regis Hotel's lobby and café and into the restaurant's intimate bar, where the wine-drinking allusions begin. Bronze-framed glass shelves hold wine bottles as well as an array of tasting glasses. Here, as in the restaurant's other rooms, Chef Ducasse's antique wine carafes punctuate the backlit display. It is the glow-in-the-dark interactive bar, however, that draws most of the media attention. (Naturally—how can a writer avoid this piece of fun?) A conventional wine list may seem more practi-

cal. However, the touch-activated technology is more cutting-edge.

The formal restaurant lies just beyond the darkened, sexy bar. Color cues drawn from the wine world set the tone in the inner dining sanctum. Champagne and Burgundy are natural choices. A grape pattern is etched on the glass veil wall in the main dining room, and handblown glass bubbles hang from the ceilings. But the overarching design statement is made by the four giant temperature-controlled armoires showcasing some of Adour's vast collection of international wines throughout the dining room. Rockwell customized the armoires, which were manufactured by York Street Studios. In a move that surpasses those for most residential projects, the wine lockers' interiors were velvet-lined, made with aubergine burled mahogany and antique bronze fittings.

Says Rockwell, "Adour Alain Ducasse at the St. Regis is a celebration of the richness, complexity, and character of wine, exhibited through the crafted palette and materials. It is a story of contrasts, such as the layering of cutting-edge wine technology with traditional sommelier service, and the wrapping of the historic

A leather-clad bar area provides an interactive glow-in-the-dark wine list projected directly onto the surface.

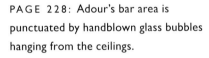

PAGE 228: Adour's bar area is punctuated by handblown glass bubbles hanging from the ceilings.

ABOVE: VIPs can store favorites in sleek storage bins designed by Rockwell especially for Adour.

OPPOSITE: The formal restaurant interiors and architecture are clearly inspired by the wine world. Its colors are champagne and burgundy, and the walls are wrapped in glass decorated by hand in a grape pattern.

architecture of the main dining room with a modern glass veil wall with an abstract grapevine pattern."

Do the interiors work for the chef? "It's like a Fabergé egg," Ducasse told *New York* magazine. And with the rich palette of materials, the layering, the uses of crystal—from light fixtures to decanters—and fantastic touches such as the ice buckets built into the banquettes, his analogy sings with truth.

THE HEIGHTS OF WINE

NEW YORK, NEW YORK

RESTAURANTS OFTEN IGNITE TRENDS THAT SOON TRANSLATE INTO THE HOME. Thus it comes as no surprise that the wine display at New York City's Northern Italian restaurant Alto keeps sparking the reaction "I want one!"

Soaring the height of the sixteen-foot-high ceilings, these wine cases are monolithic. Fitted with lighting that throbs like a mood ring, awash in stainless steel and glass, the structure, created by the celebrated designer Vicente Wolf, is an urbanely emotional storage solution. Creative collaboration between the restaurant's owner, Chris Cannon, and Wolf stretches back to JUdson Grill, a restaurant that in its time was referred to as the Hearst Publications cafeteria because it was a favorite of publishing folk. But Alto was the first occasion in which Wolf brought the wines out from behind the scenes and featured them in the dining room. And he won the James Beard Award for his dazzling display.

Wolf explains that when confronted by Alto's raw restaurant space, the one big issue for him was the ceiling's height, which created what could have been a hollow expanse. "The space wasn't very wide, but it was extremely tall. I thought it would be fun to construct the restaurant inside the wine cellar."

Seeking to create a sense of extreme drama, he drew inspiration for the wine cases from Damien Hirst's famous installations—which are animals preserved in formaldehyde in lucite boxes. The glass cases of wine stack 5,000 bottles. All are framed in stainless steel in a combination of high polish and satin. In a very Vegas touch, the insides of the cases are lined with lights that pulse from pink to green to blue.

The wine list is likewise daring. Its selection of 700 bottles offers nine Lagreins, which are made from the distinctive red grape of Alto Adige—the region that inspired the restaurant's cuisine—as well as a series of wines from top Bordeaux châteaux, including twenty-two different vintages of Château Latour, some dating as far back as 1928. Those important bottles are stored in a more conventional cellar below the restaurant. The towering wine cellars contain the wines that are used more generally, the less rare, and the wines that are poured by the glass.

When Wolf reinterprets the Alto concept for the home, the cellar is scaled down to a more human

Designer Wolf is inspired by
Damien Hirst's installations:
animals encased in Lucite boxes.
Frames are made of high polish
and satin stainless steel. Inside,
the cases are lined with pink,
green, and blue pulsing lights.

PAGE 234: The glass-cased wine display stretches 16 feet high and stacks 5,000 bottles.

ABOVE RIGHT: Second-floor seating offers restaurant-goers another vista of the wine wall.

height. "For a recent client I purchased five seven-foot-high wine coolers and strung them together in a horizontal row to give that sense of row upon row of bottles. And while the cellar's height might be more accessible, the wines they stored in it were spectacular."

Metal wine caves can now be spotted in residences and restaurants from Miami to New York to Las Vegas to Los Angeles. Many oenophiles, especially those whose tastes lean toward modern style, consider these innovative designs, born from high-art installations, as the new "must-haves" for racking in their wine storage spaces.

RESOURCES

PART 1:
THE ENTERTAINING PAIR'S LAIR

VIEW TO A VINEYARD

Wine Cellar Design: David Spon, Wine Cellar Concepts, MacLean, VA. 202-251-1999. Davidspon.com.

Interior Design: Diamond Baratta Design, NYC. 212-966-8892. Diamondbarattadesign.com.

Racks: White oak, by David Spon, Wine Cellar Concepts.

Photography: Sara Matthews, fabricated by Dugal Visual Solutions, NYC. 212-924-8100. Saramatthews.com.

Computer System: Apple Driven CellarTracker system, installed by Marc Lazar, Cellar Advisors, LLC, St. Louis, MO. 314-667-5328. Cellaradvisors.com.

Chandeliers: In plaster by Bourgeois Boheme, Los Angeles, CA. 323-936-7507. Bobo-antiques.com.

Table: Bronze base and French limestone top, designed by Homer, NYC. 212-744-7705. Homerdesign.com.

Rug: Handwoven Himalayan wool, designed by Gene Meyer, Niba Rug Collections, Miami, FL. 305-573-1355. Nibarugs.com.

Wall of Wine Bottles: Jean Shin, Frederieke Taylor Gallery, NYC. 646-230-0992. Frederieketaylorgallery.com; Jeanshin.com.

Wine bottle mosaic (Objects of Desire sidebar): Studium, NYC. 212-486-1811. Studium.com.

MOROCCAN MOODS

Interior Design: Celerie Kemble, Kemble Interiors Inc., NYC. 212-675-9576. Kembleinteriors.com.

Architect: Peter Cadoux, Cadoux Architects, Westport, CT. 203-227-4304. Cadouxaia.com.

A MAP OF ITALY

Wine Cellar Design: Lee Zinser, Cellarworks, Inc., NYC. 212-734-9463; Beverly Hills, CA. 310-402-2099. Cellarworks.com.

Interior Designers: Lori Weatherly, Cooper, Robertson & Weatherly, NYC. 212-247-1717. Crweatherly.com.

Architects: Nick Cusano, Cusano Associates, Mendham, NJ. 973-543-1292. Cusanoassociates.com.

Contractor: Larry Glidden, Gateway Construction, Bedford, NJ. 732-513-8926.

Racks: African mahogany wine storage furniture and finishes by Cellarworks, Inc., NYC. 212-734-9463; Beverly Hills, CA. 310-402-2099. Cellarworks.com.

Flooring: Stone tile from France. Artistic Tile, Paramus, NJ. 201-670-6100. Artistictile.com.

Lights: Chandeliers, Fortuny. Fortuny.com.

Decorative Painters: Painting a Dream, Florham Park, NJ. Paintingadream.com.

Complete Environmental Control and Cellar Protection System: Cellartherm, by Consolidated Cellars, LLC. 800-930-4071. Cellartherm.com.

Favorite Wine Books, Resources, Websites: *The Accidental Connoisseur*, by Lawrence Osborne; *Battle for Wine and Love*, by Alice Feiring; WineSearcher.com; Devino.com.

Stemware, Decanters: Riedel. Riedel.com.

Cooling Systems: Custom-designed split system with humidity and dehumidification controls; integrated electronic controllers, by Cellarworks, Inc. Cellarworks.com.

THE FIRST FLUSH

Wine Cellar Design: Lee Zinser, Cellarworks, Inc., NYC. 212-734-9463; Beverly Hills, CA. 310-402-2099. Cellarworks.com.

Interior Designers: Marie Aiello, Marie Aiello Design Studio, NYC. 212-988-1911. Ma-ds.com.

Racks and Wine Storage Furniture: African mahogany, Cellarworks designs, licensed by Kilter Hippo, LLC, NYC. 212-734-9463. Cellarworks.com.

Lighting: Suffolk Designer Lighting, Southampton, NY. 631-283-4800. Suffolkdesignerlighting.com.

Flooring: Chiseled and brushed travertine Noce, Cancos Tile, NYC. 212-627-1545; 800-3-CANCOS. Cancos.com.

Environmental Control and Cellar Protection System: Cellartherm, by Consolidated Cellars, LLC. 800-930-4071. Cellartherm.com.

Cooling Systems: Custom-designed split system with humidity and dehumidification controls and integrated electronic controllers, custom by Cellarworks, Inc.

Wine Cave Columns: Jerusalem ancient wall stone limestone, Walker Zanger, NYC. 212-844-3000. Walkerzanger.com.

Wine Cave Backsplash: Durango Limestone, Nemo Tile, NYC. 212-505-0009; 800-NEMO-TILE. Nemotile.com.

Backsplash: Polished Honey Onyx Mosaic, Nemo Tile, NYC. 212-505-0009; 800-NEMO-TILE. Nemotile.com

Bar and Countertops: Polished Chocolate Lab Marble, Artistic Tile. 877-528-5401. Artistictile.com.

Lounge Carpet: Missoni Palermo in Saddle, Stark, NYC. 212-752-9000. Starkcarpet.com.

Gallery Floor: Exobam Okan prefinished hardwood on bamboo substrate, Architectural Systems, Inc., NYC. 212-206-1730. archsystems.com.

Bar and Wine Cave Hot Rolled Steel: Edelman Metal Works, Inc., Danbury, CT. 860-355-7525.

Hardware: Satin nickel with chocolate leather recesses, Turnstyle Designs for Gracious Home, NYC. 800-338-7809. Gracioushome.com.

Stemware, Decanters: Collection of Riedel and other decanters. Riedel.com.

Audio-Visual System: Crestron system, Entertainment Technologies, Dallas, TX. 800-223-9477. Etdimming.com.

NARRAGANSETT STYLE

Wine Cellar Design: Fred Tregaskis, New England Wine Cellars, LLC, Falls Village, CT. 800-863-4851. Newcellars.com.

Interior Design: Ramona Rodger, Lifestyle Designs in Newport, RI. 401-619-2900.

Architect: Richard R. Hunt Architect, LTD., West Greenwich, RI. 401-397-9309.

Furniture: Furnitureland South, Jamestown, NC. 336-822-3000. Furniturelandsouth.com.

Wing Chairs: Barrett Chair, Bentley Churchill, Taylorsville, NC. 828-635-1860. Bentleychurchill.com.

Sectional Sofa: Bentley Churchill, Taylorsville, NC. 828-635-1860. Bentleychurchill.com.

Coffee Table: Hunt Club Mahogany Cocktail Table, Maitland-Smith, High Point, NC. Maitland-smith.com.

Small Stools: Emperor Stool, South Cone, Poway, CA. 619-299-2038. Southcone.com.

Bar Stools: Hancock & Moore, Hickory, NC. Hancockandmoore.com.

Bar: English oak, Van Millwork, Fitchburg, MA. 979-353-7775. Vanmillwork.com.

Sliding Barn Doors: Van Millwork, Fitchburg, MA. 979-353-7775. Vanmillwork.com.

Floors: Ash with English oak inlays, installed by Tim Newman, Pride Flooring, Mashpee, MA. 508-420-8727. Prideflooringinc.com.

Tile and Brick: Installed by Kenneth Castellucci & Associates, Lincoln, RI. 401-333-5400. Castellucci.com.

Stone: Carnelian granite, installed by Kenneth Castellucci & Associates, Lincoln, RI. 401-333-5400. Castellucci.com.

Metalwork on Barn Doors: Cape Cod Fabricators, North Falmouth, MA. 508-564-5777.

Glass: Antique, The Stained Glass Emporium, Rehoboth, MA. 508-336-5455.

Stemware: Marquis, by Waterford. 800-955-1550.
Waterford.com.

Lighting: Mancini Lighting, East Greenwich, RI.
401-886-9125. Mancinilighting.com.

ASIAN FLAIR

Wine Cellar Design: Fred Tregaskis, New England Wine
Cellars, LLC, Falls Village, CT. 800-863-4851.
Newcellars.com.

Interior Design: Kelly Hoppen Interiors, London. 011-44-20-
7471-3350. Kellyhoppenretail.com.

Architects: Rebecca Rasmussen, Rasmussen Architects, Inc.,
NYC. 212-362-9546. Rasmussenarchitects.com.

Flooring: Poured concrete in Sandstone finish, ZEN
Associates, Inc., Washington, DC. 800-834-6654.
Zenassociates.com.

Wood, Glass Doors: Southern Exposure Sunrooms,
Wilmington, NC. 910-793-2762.
Southernexposuresunrooms.com.

Hardware: Rocky Mountain Hardware, Hailey, ID. 208-788-
2013. Rockmountainhardware.com; Baldwin Hardware,
800-566-1986. Baldwinhardware.com. Katonah
Hardware, Katonah, NY. 914-232-7796.
Katonahhardware.com.

Copper Counters: New England Wine Cellars, LLC, Falls
Village, CT. 800-863-4851. Newcellars.com.

Cooling Systems: CellarMate, Falls Village, CT. 888-564-
2932. Cellarmate.com.

DESIGNED FOR LIVING

Cellar Design: Ben Benoit, Cellar Masters, Los Angeles, CA.
805-375-5092. Cellarmastersinc.com.

PART II:
THE GENTLEMAN'S HAVEN

ROYAL TREATMENT

Wine Cellar Design: David Spon, Wine Cellar Concepts,
MacLean, VA. 202-251-1999. Davidspon.com.

Designer: Ellie Cullman, Cullman & Kravis, Inc., NYC.
212-294-3874. Cullmankravis.com.

Architect: Elliott Rosenblum, Rosenblum Architects, NYC.
212-352-0001. Rosenblumarchitects.com.

Linens, Horn Accessories, Cheese Plates: Sandra Jordan,
Healdsburg, CA. 707-836-9240. Sandrajordan.com.

WINE IN HIS BLOOD

Wine Cellar Design: Lee Zinser, Cellarworks, Inc., NYC.
212-734-9463. Beverly Hills, CA. 310-402-2099.
Cellarworks.com.

Interior Design: Matthew Isom, MILC Design, NYC. 917-
714-6968. Matt@milcdesign.com.

Custom Furniture: Matthew Isom, MILC Design, NYC. 917-
714-6968. Matt@milcdesign.com.

Architect: Lisa RE Zaloga Architect, Southampton, NY.
631-283-8228.

Racks and Museum Display Island: Rare koa wood species,
custom-designed by Cellarworks, Inc., NYC. 212-734-
9463; Beverly Hills, CA. 310-402-2099. Cellarworks.com.

Security System: Biometric access control, ACTAtek. 800-
400-9292. Acatekusa.com.

Environmental Control and Protection System: Cellartherm,
by Consolidated Cellars, LLC. 800-930-4071.
Cellartherm.com.

Wine Storage Furniture: Cellarworks designs, licensed by
Kilter Hippo, LLC, NYC. 212-734-9463. Cellarworks.com.

Stemware: WMF, Farmingdale, NY. 631-293-3990. Wmf.com.

Cooling Systems: Custom-designed split system with humidity and dehumidification controls, Cellarworks, Inc., NYC. 212-734-9463; Beverly Hills, CA. 310-402-2099. Cellarworks.com.

Favorite Wine Stores, Websites: Sherry-Lehmann, sherry-lehmann.com; Sokolin & Co., Sokolin.com; Wine exchange, Winex.com; Acker Merrall & Condit, Ackerwines.com.

THE NATURAL

Wine Cellar Design: Patrick Wallen, Artistic Wine Cellars, San Rafael, CA. 415-492-1450. Artisticcellars.com.

Racks, Peninsual Bridges: Unfinished redwood, Artistic Wine Cellars, San Rafael, CA. 415-492-1450. Artisticcellars.com.

Lighting: LHR displays, custom-designed arch, and in-rack lighting, Artistic Wine Cellars, San Rafael, CA. 415-492-1450. Artisticcellars.com.

Floors: Handmade concrete countertops and floors inlaid with grape and leaf patterns, Artistic Wine Cellars, San Rafael, CA. 415-492-1450. Artisticcellars.com.

Inventory System: Scanning labels track inventory, Artistic Wine Cellars, San Rafael, CA. 415-492-1450. Artisticcellars.com.

WOODEN WONDERLAND

Wine Cellar Design: Thomas Warner, Thomas E. Warner Wine Cellar Company, Novato, CA. 415-883-8120. Thomaswarnerwinecellars.com.

Racks: Aged distressed walnut, Thomas E. Warner Wine Cellar Company, Novato, CA. 415-883-8120. Thomaswarnerwinecellars.com.

Lighting: All display lighting within racking system, Thomas E. Warner Wine Cellar Company, Novato, CA. 415-883-8120. Thomaswarnerwinecellars.com.

Cooling Systems: Phil Finer Refrigeration, Redwood City, CA. 888-245-6493; 650-366-6656. Philfiner.com.

THE DAYS OF WINE AND BASEBALL

Wine Cellar Design: Fred Tregaskis, New England Wine Cellars, LLC, Falls Village, CT. 800-863-4851. Newcellars.com.

Interior Design: Barbara Kotzen, Tappe & Kotzen Interior Design, LLP, Wellesley, MA. 781-235-1740.

Architect: Thomas Catalano, Catalano Architects, Inc., Boston, MA. 617-338-7447. Catalanoinc.com.

Chandeliers: Ironware International, NYC. 800-850-0460; 615-726-2500. Ironwareinternational.com.

Flooring and Walls: Travertine limestone, Discover Tile, LLC, Boston, MA. 617-330-7900. Discovertile.com.

Door Hardware: Rocky Mountain Hardware, Hailey, ID. 208-788-2013. Rockymountainhardware.com.

Stemware and Decanters: Simon Pearce. 800-774-5227. Simonpearce.com.

Favorite Wine Stores and Websites: Fifth Avenue Liquors, Framingham, MA. 508-872-7777. Fifthaveliquor.com.

Builder: Mark Cahill, Cahill Development Corp., Weston, MA. 617-633-0555. Cahilldevelopmentcorp.com.

A SOPHISTICATED PASSION

Wine Cellar Design: Ben Benoit, Cellar Masters, Inc., Newbury Park, CA. 805-375-5040. Cellarmastersinc.com.

Architect: David E. Martin, David E Martin Architects, Los Angeles, CA.

Lighting and Flooring: Jeffrey Alan Marks, Inc., Santa Monica, CA. 310-207-2222. Jam-design.com.

Stone Table: Jeffrey Alan Marks, Inc., Santa Monica, CA. 310-207-2222. Jam-design.com.

Racks and Cooling System: Cellar Masters, Newbury Park, CA. 805-375-5040. Cellarmastersinc.com.

General Contractor: Richard F. Crawford, The Richard F. Crawford Company, Costa Mesa, CA. 714-545-0904.

RENAISSANCE MAN

Interior Design: Jeff Andrews Design, Los Angeles, CA. 323-227-9777. Jeffandrews-design.com.

Wine Cellar Design: Jean-Marie France Mercier, TIXA Wine Cellars, Los Angeles, CA. 323-650-1829. Tixawinecellars. com.

Contractor: Simmonds Builders, Van Nuys, CA. 818-780-9834.

Racks: Clear Heart Redwood, TIXA Wine Cellars, Los Angeles, CA. 323-650-1829. Tixawinecellars.com.

Hanging Pendants: Pasadena Antique Center, Pasadena, CA. 626-396-0843. Pasadenaantiquecenter.com.

Custom Ceiling Mount Fixtures: Jeff Andrews, fabricated by Pasadena Lighting, Inc., Pasadena, CA. 626-564-1112. Lightingexterior.com.

Tiles: Maison Francaise terra-cotta, Walker Zanger, West Hollywood, CA. 310-659-1234. Walkerzanger.com.

Cabinetry: Hardwood mahogany, by Woodmaster Furniture, Inc., Burbank, CA. 818-847-2130.

Hardware: Ashley Norton, Details, West Hollywood, CA. 310-659-1550; Pompton Plains, N.J. 800-393-1097. Ashleynorton.com.

Stemware: Riedel. Riedel.com.

Favorite Wine Accessories Store: Table Art, Los Angeles, CA. 323-653-8278, Tartontheweb.com; Ok Store, Los Angeles, CA. 323-653-3501. Okstore.la.

Chairs: Antique barrel chairs, J. F. Chen, Los Angeles, CA. 323-466-9700. Jfchen.com.

Painting: Vintage abstract painting, J. F. Chen, Los Angeles, CA. 323-466-9700. Jfchen.com.

PART III: THE SYBARITE'S SANCTUARY

ODE TO SAKE

Interior Designer: Alexa Hampton, Mark Hampton Inc., NYC. 212-753-4110. Markhampton.com.

Wine Cellar Design: Lee Zinser, Cellarworks, Inc., NYC. 212-734-9463; Beverly Hills, CA. 310-402-2099. Cellarworks.com.

Racks: African mahogany wine storage furniture and finishes, Cellarworks designs licensed by Kilter Hippo, NYC. 212-734-9463. Cellarworks.com.

Lighting: Cellarworks, NYC. 212-734-9463. Beverly Hills, CA. 310-402-2099. Cellarworks.com.

Environmental Control and Cellar Protection System: Cellartherm, by Consolidated Cellars, LLC. 800-930-4071. Cellartherm.com.

Stemware: Riedel, Sommelier. Riedel.com.

Refrigerated Storage Units: Vinotheque, Culver City, CA. 310-482-3490. Vinotheque.com.

Cooling Systems: Custom-designed split system with humidity and dehumidification controls; integrated electronic controllers, Cellarworks, NYC. 212-734-9463; Beverly Hills, CA. 310-402-2099. Cellarworks.com.

Security: Biometric fingerprint access, Actatek. 866-400-9292. Actatekusa.com.

Favorite Websites: Wine Enthusiast, Wineenthusiast.com; Winelibrary.com; Crush.com; Erobertparker.com; Vinfolio.com.

GOING GREEN

Wine Cellar Design: Thomas Warner, Thomas E. Warner Wine Cellar Company, Novato, CA. 415-883-8120 x3577. Thomaswarnerwinecellars.com.

Racks: Aged, distressed redwood, Thomas E. Warner Wine Cellar Company, Novato, CA. 415-883-8120. Thomaswarnerwinecellars.com.

Lighting: All display lighting within racking system, Thomas E. Warner Wine Cellar Company, Sausalito, CA. 415-883-8120 x3577. Thomaswarnerwinecellars.com.

THE MAN CAVE

Cellar Design: Ben Benoit, Cellar Masters, Newbury Park, CA. 805-375-5092. Cellarmastersinc.com.

THE CATHEDRAL OF WINE

Wine Cellar Design: Howard Backen, Backen Gillam Architects, Sausalito, CA. 415-289-3860; St. Helena, CA. 707-967-1920. Bgarch.com.

Architects: Howard Backen, Backen Gillam Architects, Sausalito, CA. 415-289-3860; St. Helena, CA. 707-967-1920. Bgarch.com. Jessie Whitesides, A-Squared Studios, Santa Rosa, CA. 707-569-9358. Asquaredstudios.com.

Interior Designers: April Powers and Joshua Rowland, Backen Gillam Architects, Sausalito, CA. 415-289-3860; St. Helena, CA. 707-967-1920. Bgarch.com.

Lighting: Bell-jar glass pendants, Holly Hunt. Hollyhunt.com.

Chandelier: Tobias Wong for Schonbek. Schonbek.com.

Recessed Accent Lights: Low-voltage adjustable, Iris Lighting Systems, a brand of Cooper Lighting, Peachtree City, GA. Iris-lighting.com.

Indirect Lighting: Xenflex linear lighting, Starfire Lighting, Woodridge, NJ. 800-443-8823. Starfirelighting.com.

Wine Niche Lighting: ABEO voltage down lights, CSL Lighting, City of Industry, CA. 626-336-4511. Csllighting.com.

Decorative Painters: Custom-color Marmorino plaster, Klein Plastering, St. Helena, CA. 707-963-1227.

Hardware: Doors and windows, Rocky Mountain Hardware, Hailey, ID. 208-788-2013. Rockymountainhardware.com.

THE LUXE LIFE

Interior Design: Michael Whaley Interiors, Inc., North Stamford, CT. 203-595-9845. Michaelwhaleyinteriors.com.

Architects: Scott Raissis, Thompson Raissis Architects, LLC, Stamford, CT. 203-399-0100. Tr-architects.com.

Wine Racks: French oak, Fairfield Hardwood Supply, Fairfield, CT. 203-362-2161. Fairfieldhardwoodsupply.com.

Lighting: Nineteenth-century French iron and bronze chandelier, William Word Fine Antiques, Atlanta, GA . 404-233-6890. Williamwordantiques.com.

Andalusian Sconces: 20th Century Lighting, Kansas City, MO. 816-421-2125. 20thcenturylighting.com.

Antique Three-Light French Iron Chandelier: Edgar Reeves, Atlanta, GA. 404-237-1137. Edgar-reeves.com.

Flooring: Limestone Greenwich Tile and Marble, Greenwich, CT. 203-869-1709.

Limestone Ceiling Tiles: Greenwich Tile and Marble, Greenwich, CT. 203-869-1709.

Decorative Painter: through Michael Whaley Interiors, Inc., North Stamford, CT. 203-595-9845. Michaelwhaleyinteriors.com.

Hardware: Top Knobs USA, Bell Meade, NJ. 800-499-9095. topknobsusa.com.

Antique Stemware, Antique Decanters, Silver Wine Coasters, Silver Trays, Biscuit Barrels: Georgina Jay Antiques, Portobello Road, London. Georginajayantiques.com; Jerome V. Jacalone Antiques, NYC. 212-838-9118; KM Antiques of London, Ltd. NYC. 212-888-7950; The London Silver Vaults, London. 011-44-20-7242-3844. Thesilvervaults.co.uk.

Refrigerators: SubZero. 800-222-7820. Subzero.com.

Favorite Place to Shop for Wine Accessories: The London Silver Vaults, London. 011-44-20-7242-3844. Thesilvervaults.co.uk.

Favorite Wine Stores: Zachy's Wine, Scarsdale, NY. 800-723-0241. Zachys.com.

PART IV: THE MODERNIST REFUGE

DIVINE ART DECO

Architects: Jacunski Humes Architect, Berlin, CT. 860-828-9221.

Wine Cellar Design: Lee Zinser, Cellarworks, Inc., NYC. 212-734-9463. Beverly Hills, CA. 310-402-2099. Cellarworks.com.

Racks: Hand-selected American cherry, Cellarworks design, licensed by Kilter Hippo, NYC. Kilter Hippo, NYC. 800-732-0372. Cellarworks.com.

Wine Storage Furniture: Kilter Hippo, NYC. 800-732-0372. Cellarworks.com.

Lighting: Bellacor. 877-723-5522. Bellacor.com.

Ceiling Fixture: Presidio Tryne Flush Ceiling Light, Bellacor. 877-723-5522. Bellacor.com.

Sconces: Antique brass ADA Wall Sconce, Bellacor. 877-723-5522. Bellacor.com.

Floor and Wall Tiles: Copper- and metal-plated tiles, Cellarworks, NYC. 212-734-9463. Beverly Hills, CA. 310-402-2099. Cellarworks.com.

Decorative Painters: Hand-rubbed parchment, Doherty Painting & Construction, San Francisco, CA. 415-695-1494.

Cellar Protection System: Cellartherm, by Consolidated Cellars, LLC. 800-930-4071. Cellartherm.com.

Construction Contractor: Doherty Painting & Construction, San Francisco, CA. 415-695-1494. Dohertypaint-const.com.

Artwork and Framing: Michael W. Perry & Company, San Francisco, CA. 415-563-8853. Mwperry.com.

Gate and Door Design: Marilyn Kuksht, Santa Cruz, CA. 831-426-1935. Kuksht.com.

Stemware, Decanters: Vinum Extreme; Cornetto decanter, Riedel. Riedel.com.

Cooling Systems: Custom-designed split system with humidity and dehumidification controls; electronic controllers, Cellarworks, NYC. 212-734-9463. Beverly Hills, CA. 310-402-2099. Cellarworks.com.

Home Entertainment System: World of Sound, Mill Valley, CA. 415-383-4343. Worldofsoundmarin.com.

THE CLUB ROOM

Wine Cellar Designer: Thomas Warner, Thomas E. Warner Wine Cellar Company, Novato, CA. 415-883-8120 x3577. Thomaswarnerwinecellars.com.

Racks: Honduran mahogany with stain and finish, Thomas E. Warner Wine Cellar Company, Novato, CA. 415-883-8120 x3577. Thomaswarnerwinecellars.com.

Lighting: All display lighting within racking system, Thomas E. Warner Wine Cellar Company, Novato, CA. 415-883-8120 x3577. Thomaswarnerwinecellars.com.

THE ISLAND CELLAR

Wine Cellar Design: Dionysi Grevenitis, DALST Stone Wine Cellars, Roxbury, NY. 718-369-0019. Dalst.com; Evan Goldberg, Design Built Constultans, Inc., Greenwich, CT. 203-861-0111. Evang.com.

Architects and Interior Designer: Andrew Kotchen and Matthew Berman, Workshop/ADP, NYC. 212-273-9712. Workshopadp.com.

General Contractor: Fraker Construction, Nantucket, MA. 508-228-9501.

Racks: Cast limestone, DALST Stone Wine Cellars, Roxbury, NY. 718-369-0019.

Lighting: Recessed and surface, Lightolier, Fall River, MA. 508-679-8131. Lightolier.com.

Flooring: Sierra Negra lavastone, Coverings, ETC., Miami, FL. 305-757-6000; NYC, 212-625-9390. Coveringsetc.com.

Floor trim: Salvaged mushroom-wood planks, Antique & Vintage Woods of America, Pine Plains, NY. 800-210-6704; 518-398-0049. Antiqueandvintagewoods.com.

Refrigerator: Custom-built by Design Built Consultants, Greenwich, CT. 203-861-0111. Evang.com.

Favorite Wine Resources: Wine Spectator. Winespectator.com.

Favorite Websites: Wineenthusiast.com. PAXwine.com.

AGE OF ANTIQUITY

Wine Cellar Design: Dionysi Grevenitis, DALST Stone Wine Cellars, Roxbury, NY. 718.369.0019. dalst.com; Evan Goldberg, Design Built Constultants, Inc., Greenwich, CT. 203-861-0111. Evang.com.

Interior Designer: Samuel Botero, Samuel Botero Associates Inc., NYC. 212-935-5155. Botero.com.

Racks: Cast limestone, blackened steel display bins, blackened steel-turned radius corners, DALST Stone Wine Cellars, Roxbury, NY. 718.369.0019.

Lighting: David Easton wall sconce in deep patina bronze, Robert Abbey, Inc. Hickory, North Carolina. 828-322-3480. Robertabbey.corporatepo.com.

Flooring: Italian porcelain tecnoquartz and travertine in Scabas, Catco Marble and Granite, Port Reading, NJ. 732-602-9600. Catcomarble.com.

Vases: Three-hundred-year-old amphorae from Erzurum, Turkey, Miranna Finds, NYC. 917-838-3266. Mirannafinds.com.

Wall Cladding: Travertine stone, A & K Tile Studio, Brooklyn, NY. 718-369-6873. Aktilestudio.com.

Double Doors: Blackened steel, custom-designed by Ferra Designs, Brooklyn, NY. 718-852-8629. Ferradesigns.com.

Console, Table, and Stools: Custom hand-wrought by Ferra Designs, Brooklyn, NY. 718-852-8629. Ferradesigns.com.

Stone Moldings: Crown, chair rail, door casing, and baseboard, The Complete Tile Collection, NYC. 212-255-4450. Completetilecollection.com.

Bronze Grilles: Architectural Grille, Brooklyn, NY. 800-387-6267. Archgrille.com.

Favorite Wine Shop: Sip Fine Wine, Brooklyn, NY. 718-638-6105. Sipfinewine.com.

VEGAS DELIGHT

Wine Cellar Design: Ben Benoit, Cellar Masters, Newbury Park, CA. 805-375-5092. Cellarmastersinc.com.

Interior Designer: Richard H. King, AICP, Karen Butera Inc., Corona Del Mar, CA. 949-640-1300. Karenbutera.com.

Contractor: Jack Raftery, Raftery Construction, Las Vegas, NV. 702-242-4475.

Glass Doors: National Glass, & Mirror, Inc., Las Vegas, NV. 702-362-3621.

Metal Work: Custom industrial sheet metal, Oxnard, CA. 805-983-3701. Customemetalinc.com.

PART V: URBAN RETREATS AND INSPIRING SPACES

CHELSEA GIRL

Cellar Design: Songal Designs, South Kent, CT. 860-927-1346.

Architects: Rene Gonzales; design associate, Amparo Vollert, Rene Gonzales Architect, Miami, FL. 305-762-5895. renegonzalesarchitect.com.

THE BACHELOR ENTHUSIAST

Wine Cellar Design: Fred Tregaskis, New England Wine Cellars LLC, Falls Village, CT. 800-863-4851. Newcellars.com.

Interior Designer: Scott Salvator, NYC. 212-861-5355. Scottsalvator.com.

Favorite Wine Shop: Gasbarro's, Providence, RI. 401-421-4170. Gasbarros.com.

ZEN CLOSET

Wine Cellar Design: Nicole Sassaman, Los Angeles, CA. 310-860-0806. Nicolesassaman.com.

Racks: Custom-made solid walnut, designed by Nicole Sassaman, Los Angeles, CA. 310-860-0806. Nicolesassaman.com.

Flooring: Custom-made 8-inch-wide, solid walnut wood planks, Nicole Sassaman, Los Angeles, CA. 310-860-0806. Nicolesassaman.com.

Stemware, Decanters: Calvin Klein. Calvinklein.com.

Favorite Wine Shop: The Wine Merchant, Beverly Hills, CA. 310-278-7322. Beverlyhillswinemerchant.com.

CLUB PARADISE

Wine Cellar Design: Backen Gillam Architects, Sausalito, CA. 415-289-3860; St. Helena, CA. 707-967-1920. Bgarch.com.

Architects: Howard Backen, Backen Gillam Architects, Sausalito, CA. 415-289-3860; St. Helena, CA. 707-967-1920. Bgarch.com.

Jessie Whitesides, A-Squared Studios, Santa Rosa, CA. 707-589-9358. San Diego, CA. 619-688-2606. Asquaredstudios.com.

Interior Designers: April Powers and Joshua Rowland, Backen Gillam Architects, Sausalito, CA. 415-289-3860; St. Helena, CA. 707-967-1920. Bgarch.com.

Limestone Racking System: Dionysi Grevenitis, DALST Stone Wine Cellars, Roxbury, NY. 718-369-0019. Dalst.com.

Stylist: Joshua Rowland, of Backen Gillam, Sausalito, CA. 415-289-3860; St. Helena, CA. 707-967-1920. Bgarch.com.

Lighting: Custom pendants by Copper Iron Designs, Napa, CA. 707-252-1949. Copperirondesigns.com.

Furniture: Copper Dining Table by Custom Furniture Design, San Francisco, CA. 415-431-1511. Customfurnituredesign.com.

Slipcover Fabrics: DeLany & Long, LTD., Greenwich, CT. 203-532-0010. Delanyandlong.com.

Drapery Fabrics: Perennials Fabrics, Dallas, TX. 214-638-4162. Perennialsfabrics.com.

Carpet: Plynyl, Ikat in Walnut, Chilewich, NYC. 212-679-9204. Chilewich.com.

THE HEIGHTS OF WINE

Interior Design: Vicente Wolf, Vicente Wolf Associates, Inc., NYC. 212-465-0590. Vicentewolf.com.

Fabrics and All Upholstered Products: VW Home by Vicente Wolf Associates, Inc., NYC. 212-244-5008. Vicentewolf.com.

All fittings: designed by Vicente Wolf and custom created for Vicente Wolf Associates, Inc., NYC. 212-244-5008. Vicentewolf.com.

WRAPPED IN WINE

Architecture and Design: David Rockwell, Shawn Sullivan, Sally Weinand, Thom Ortiz, Rich Kinnard, Rockwell Group, NYC. 212-463-0334. Rockwellgroup.com.

Lighting: Johnson Light Studio, NYC. 212-868-5204. Johnsonlightstudio.com.

Chandelier, Lamps, and Sconces: Barovier & Toso, Milano, Italy. 011-39-027-600-0906. Barovier.com.

Carpets: Custom-designed silk and wool with light and dark burgundy diamonds, Rockwell Group. Fabricated by J.S.L. Carpet Corporation, NYC. 212-751-3111. Jslcarpetcorp.com.

Wood Floors in Wine Bar: Moabe and afromosia wood floors, layout and pattern custom-designed by Rockwell Group, NYC. 212-463-0334. Rockwellgroup.com.

Technology: Custom-designed interactive wine bar and private vault room, Rockwell Group in collaboration with Potion, NYC. 718-388-5263. Potiondesign.com.

Goatskin Bar Top, Leather Wine Vaults: Custom-designed, Rockwell Group; fabricated by York Street Studio, New Milford, CT. 860-350-5559. Yorkstreet.com.

Host Stand and Bar in Wine Bar Area: Custom-designed, Rockwell Group; cast by James Vilona, Boulder, CO. 303-444-2363. Jamesvilona.com.

Flecked Glass Spheres in Wine Bar Area and Private Vault Dining Room: Ken Gangbar Studios, Toronto, Canada. 416-532-4284. Kengangbar.com.

Makore Wood Walls: Patella Woodworking, NYC. 212-414-9161. Patellawoodworking.com.

Laminated Grapevine Pattern in Antique Glass Veil Wall: Custom-designed, Rockwell Group; fabricated by Casey Maher, NYC. 917.405.9307. Thiswillkillthat.com.

Leafing on Walls: In Platinum by Evergreene Painting Studios, Inc., NYC. 212-244-2800. Evergreene.com.

Cast Glass Table Tops: Galaxy Glass, Fairfield, NJ. 973-575-3440. Galaxycustom.com.

Mercury Mirrors on Ceiling in Side Dining Rooms: Pin Antique Gold, Port Richmond Glass, NYC. 212-269-2433. Portrichmondglass.com.

Chairs and Banquettes: Bright Chair Company, NYC. 212-726-9030. Brightchair.com.

Decanting Station: Solid moabe wood with bent-glass splatter guard, G.E.R. Industries Inc., New Rochelle, NY. 914-633-3118.

Corner Banquette Leather: Roger Arlington Leather, Inc., NYC. 212-752-5288.

Decorative Painting: Adour River Mural, by Nancy Lorenz, NYC. 212-989-1354.

WEBSITES

Alicefeiring.com

Crush.com

Devino.com

Erobertparker.com

Landmarkwine.com (wine club)

Montesquieuwine.com

Montesquieuwinebrokers.com

PAXwine.com

Rarewineco.com

Vinfolio.com

Wineenthusiast.com

Winelibrary.com

Wine-searcher.com

Winespectator.com

Zachys.com

WINE SHOPS

Acker, Merrall & Condit, NYC. 212-787-1700.
   Ackermerrall.org.

Bottle Rocket Wine & Spirit, NYC. 212-929-2323.
   Bottlerocket.com.

Chelsea Wine Vault, NYC. 212-462-4244.
   Chelseawinevault.com.

De Vino, NYC. 212-228-0073. De-vino.com.

Fifth Avenue Liquors, Framingham, MA. 508-872-7777.
   Fifthaveliquor.com.

Gasbarro's, Providence, RI. 401-421-4170. Gasbarros.com

Grapes & Gourmet, Jamestown, RI. 401-423-0070.

Hart Davis Hart Wine Co., Chicago, IL. 312-482-9996.
   Johnhartfinewine.com.

Italian Wine Merchants, NYC. 212-473-2323.
   Italianwinemerchant.com.

James Robinson, 480 Park Avenue, New York, NY 10022;
   212-752-6166.

Morrell Wine, NYC. 212-688-9370. Morrellwine.com.

Sam's Wine & Spirits, Chicago, IL. 877-342-3611.
   Samswine.com.

Sherry-Lehmann, NYC. 212-838-7500. Sherry-lehmann.com.

Sip Fine Wine, Brooklyn, NY. 718-638-6105. Sipfinewine.com

The Wine Merchant, Beverly Hills, CA. 310-278-7322.
   Beverlyhillswinemerchant.com.

Vestry Wines, NYC. 212-810-2899. Vestrywines.com.

Wine Legend, Livingston, NJ. 973-992-4441.
   Winelegend.com.

Zachy's, NY. 800-723-0241. Zachys.com.

WINE ACCESSORIES

Italian Wine Merchants, NYC.

Orrefors. 011-46-4813-4000. Orrefors.com.

Riedel. Riedel.com.

Sandra Jordan Collection, LLC. Healdsburg, CA. 707-433-
   3311. Sandrajordan.com.

Simon Pearce. Simonpearce.com.

Spiegelau. Spiegelau.com.

Table Art, Los Angeles, CA. 323-653-8278.

The London Silver Vaults, London. 011-44-20-7242-3844.
   Thesilvervaults.com.

Wineenthusiast.com.

AUCTION HOUSES

Bonhams & Butterfields. Bonhams.com.

Brentwood Wine Company, LLC. West Linn, Oregon.
   503-638-9463. Brentwoodwine.com.

Christie's. Christies.com.

Edward Roberts International, Chicago, IL. 847-295-8696.
   Eriwine.com.

Sotheby's. Sothebys.com.

WINE FESTIVALS

Aspen Food & Wine Event

Boston Wine Expo

Grape Nuts

Nantucket Wine Festival

Napa Valley Wine Auction

New York Wine Experience

Sonoma County Wine Auction

South Beach Food & Wine Festival

Tanglewood Wine Festival

ACKNOWLEDGMENTS

LIVING WITH WINE would not have been possible without the hard work of a wonderful ensemble of talented professionals: my collaborators—writer Alice Feiring, photographer Andrew French, production coordinator Damaris Colhoun, and stylist Callie Jenschke.

I am deeply grateful to my editor, Aliza Fogelson, whose ultimate understanding ushered the completion of *Living with Wine*. She deserves special recognition for her patience with a new mother experiencing "the sophomore book blues."

I'd also like to thank Clarkson Potter publisher Lauren Shakely and editorial director Doris Cooper, who gave me my start at Clarkson Potter and encouraged my efforts. Thanks go to the talented Jennifer K. Beal Davis for her beautiful design. I am also appreciative for the efforts of Rachelle Mandik, Kim Tyner, Peggy Paul, and the rest of the Potter team. I'd be remiss if I did not acknowledge the designers, architects, cellar-builders, and wine collectors who provided the projects (and often shared their wines) featured in this book.

Thanks also go to my colleagues at *Metropolitan Home*—Donna Warner, Deborah Burns, Christine Boyle, and Barbara Friedmann—for allowing me to do the ultimate juggling act.

I am also indebted to my friends and family for keeping me laughing and awake as I raised my newborn, returned to work at *Metropolitan Home*, bought my dream home, and completed this book. The ever-gracious and hilarious Kirsten Brant, Monica Cheslak, Christopher Coleman, Patrick Danek, Rebecca Dreyfus, Elaine Griffin, Lisa Jasper, Janice Langrall, Bonnie Lasek, Jill Levine, Joanne Maurno, Liz Quinn, Scott Salvator, and Doug Wilson. Thanks also to my parents, Bobbi and Larry, my sister Jackie, and cousin KT (and their families) for the hours of babysitting, editing, and keeping me hydrated.

And, finally, my deepest appreciation to my husband, Michael, and son, Finn, for their understanding and endless support.

INDEX